D1142257

FANTASTIC
OPTICAL
ILLUSIONS

DEDICATION

To my hardy, timeless art professor, Felix Maurice, who taught me a lot on the illusion of art and on my unlimited ego… and whose name still puzzles me: is Felix the first or the last name?
– Gianni A. Sarcone

THIS IS A CARLTON BOOK

Text and artwork copyright © 2006, 2019 Archimedes' Laboratory™
Design copyright © 2019 Carlton Books Ltd

First published in 2006
Revised edition published in 2019 by Carlton Books Limited
20 Mortimer Street
London W1T 3JW

A CIP catalogue record for this book is available from the British Library

Editor: Georgia Goodall
Design: Andri Johannsson
Production: Jess Arvidsson

ISBN: 978-1-78739-235-9

10 9 8 7 6 5 4 3 2 1

Printed in Dubai

FANTASTIC
OPTICAL
ILLUSIONS

More than 150 deceptive
images and visual tricks

Gianni A. Sarcone & Marie-Jo Waeber

CARLTON
BOOKS

CONTENTS

INTRODUCTION

Vision is allusion

Since ancient times, humans have known that immediate perception is not a reading of physical reality. This is specifically illustrated by Plato's allegory of the cave: humans are likened to prisoners chained in a cave, unable to turn their heads and thus to see any real objects. All they can see are shadows of objects projected by a light source on the wall of the cave. What the prisoners perceive, therefore, are just shadows and echoes cast by objects that they do not see at all. Such prisoners would mistake appearance (shadows) for reality.

But what is seeing? What is vision? What is the visual experience? Vision is the most creative act that a human being is capable of. Seeing is depicting the world on the living canvas of our mind. As we depict well only what we really know, our mind is both the canvas and the artist. In this creative process, the eyes represent nothing other than a medium with which our mind interprets and 'reconstructs' the reality around us. The poet Novalis said: "the eyes are a 'superficial' organ". In fact, we will never perceive the real world because it is strongly dependent of our body and our mind. Yes, vision isn't quite

the 100 per cent natural process that folk may think… It relies for a large part on learned skills that are helpful in interpreting our near environment, but can sometimes deceive. That's why the study of visual illusions and mental fallacies is important: they reveal the magic and the limits of our perception (or consciousness). Some illusions teach us to doubt and to question the many appearances of the reality – they are a kind of school for life.

When you look in the mirror, the person in front of you, even though you are used to them, isn't really you. It is an alien with the heart on the right and the liver on the left. How much imagination do we need to understand how we truly perceive ourselves and how others perceive us? Try this experiment: scan a photo of yourself and, with the help of photo retouching software, flip it horizontally to create a mirror image and print it. Now compare this image with the original photo. Which of the two faces do you prefer? Show both images to a friend, and ask which version he or she prefers. You will probably prefer the mirror image and your friend the 'normal' version. It's a question of habit – we prefer that which we are used to… Two visions of the same person! But the illusion is also of the mind; especially when we believe we can control our thoughts. Try NOT thinking of a polar bear. Did you manage it, or did the polar bear lumber slowly into your mind? Now try to think of a green, green man and think quickly of a number from 1 to 5... Then a number from 5 to 10. We bet you thought of 3 and 7? Another example is when imagination and will 'collide' – it is always imagination which leads the way. It is easy to walk across a board laid flat on the ground but, with all the will in the world, quite impossible to walk the same plank suspended between two buildings ten floors up. The consciousness is one of the greatest mysteries of the brain. Many actions – walking, catching the bus, answering the phone – are performed unconsciously and we only become aware of them after they are completed. A recent study has revealed that our conscious decision to move a limb is done roughly one second after the area of the brain has activated the movement. Therefore, is it ourselves who control our own behavior, or is free will an illusion created by our brains? Illusions, always illusions... We are immersed in a sea of mental illusions: illusions of certainty, illusions of security...

What actually are optical or visual illusions? In the fewest words, they are illusions that deceive the human visual

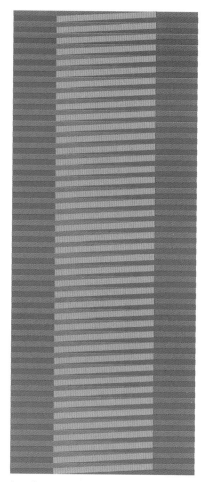

Just Gray...
Color experiment with gray lines... What happens is called color assimilation: the gray color appears bluish in contact with blue, and orange-colored in contact with orange, giving the impression of a color gradation.

system into perceiving something that is not present or incorrectly perceiving what is present. Optical illusions can be categorized as: **physical**, **physiological** and **cognitive**. Physical illusions are phenomenal illusions that occur before light enters the eye, such as a mirage, a rainbow or a straw in a glass of water. Physiological illusions are the effects on the eyes or brain of prolonged stimulation of a specific type: brightness, tilt, color, movement. Cognitive illusions interact with different levels of perceptual processing, and in-built assumptions or 'knowledge' are misdirected. Cognitive illusions are commonly divided into ambiguous, distorting, and paradoxical illusions.

Optical illusions have been studied for millennia. Even our prehistoric ancestors may have been puzzled by visual illusions, although they didn't leave traces of it... They must surely have noticed and experienced some visual phenomena, such as:

– the after-image effect on their eyes, when looking into the sun;

– a stick that seems broken when half of it is put in water;

– the Moon illusion (the rising Moon seems twice as large as the Moon in the zenith);

– and the natural optical phenomenon called a mirage.

The ancient Greeks used a technique known as entasis which incorporates a slight convexity in the columns of a temple to compensate for the illusion of concavity created by parallel lines (more recently, Rolls-Royce cars all made use of entasis in their radiator grills).

Over the years, many people have found uses for optical illusions. We could say that tricking people's eyes has been a way of life in art, technology and in entertainment. But why do most people like optical illusions? Perhaps because illusions look like magic or conjuring? Rod Serling once wrote: "In any quest for magic, in any search for sorcery, witchery, legerdemain, first check the human heart" (Dust). Each one of us has his own reasons for appreciating being surprised or puzzled by visual illusions: some, with a scientific instinct, love searching for the reasoning and logical explanation behind them (thinking they are smart enough to figure it out!). Some, with an artistic background, are rather attracted by the aesthetics, and others by the contemplative aspect of the illusions. It is known that people who like to be fooled by optical illusions are 'big kids'. Our opinion is that the marvel of optical illusions takes us back to the dawn of our childhood, that nostalgia that haunts every one of us.

To resume, optical illusions teach us how we perceive things – they show us the seams in the fabric of the reality we (re)create. In this book, divided into seven main topics (ambiguous figures, impossible figures, hidden figures, color perception, moving patterns, paradoxes and magic), you will find an interesting and suggestive collection of visual puzzles to solve and optical illusions to enjoy and experiment with. A large part of the illusions were invented and designed by the authors, while some others are adaptations of lesser known optical illusions or based on recent studies made by leading researchers in the field of the cognitive neurosciences, such as E. Andelson, H. Ashida, J. Faubert, G. Kanisza, A. Kitaoka, A. Logvinenko, B. Pinna and H. Van Tuijl. To complete the picture, you will find at the end of this book a catalog of historical optical illusions discovered by scientists, psychologists and artists of the nineteenth and twentieth centuries.

Each illusion, when necessary, is explained with simple and clear words – this book is intended for everyone – but please be aware that most of the explanations are empirical and based on intuitions rather than on real scientific proof. Some perceptive illusions are still under discussion and the scientists who studied these phenomena are only able to make suppositions. We have also to say that researchers sometimes have the bad habit of concealing their ignorance and build from the slightest little thing great short-lived theories that are not always consistent nor founded (who remembers the clumsy theory of right and left brain?). The best way to understand how and why an illusion works is to experience it with your friends and try constructing a variant... If the variant works, that means that you have understood the secret mechanism of the illusion. We hope that you will use our stunning illustrations as a resource and inspiration for designing and creating new optical illusions.

A

B

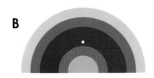

Brighten It Up
The colors of the rainbow in figure A are faded. To restore their intensity, stare at the white dot in figure B for 20–30 seconds, then shift your gaze back to figure A. This effect is based on color adaptation.

In conclusion, dear Reader, all the world is a stage, but there is always an unexpected curtain to rise. Enjoy!

Gianni A. Sarcone
Marie-Jo Waeber

"Everything we see hides another thing; we always want to see what is hidden by what we see."
- René Magritte

Perspective, geometric and angle illusions

Our brain often translates the physical image we perceive into an image which is more useful to our senses. As you experience it in everyday life, there is a distinction between the actual size of an object, its apparent or angular size and its imaginary size. The actual size of an object cannot be observed, because in order for our eyes to focus upon that object it must be at a certain distance. But you can calculate or measure it. The perceived or angular size of an object is a measure of how large the object actually 'appears' to be and depends primarily on the visual angle subtended by the object on the retina in our eyes. All other things being equal, the object that subtends the larger visual angle will appear larger. The visual angle is dependent on the actual size of the object and on the distance the object is from our eyes. A camel may not pass through the eye of a needle, but its image – apparent size – can! Actually, it would be possible to see an 80-inch wide camel placed at a distance of 0.6 miles from you, through a two millimeter-wide eye of a needle. What about the imaginary size? Psychologically, we tend sometimes to see objects larger (or smaller) than they appear in reality. For example, it's very difficult to determine at a rough guess the real size of circular objects.

The fact that we have two eyes (binocular vision) is more than sufficient to provide information on distances, and for that reason we don't need three… One of these binocular distance cues is called convergence. Convergence refers to the turning in of our eyes as objects come closer to them (and is what causes you to have a squint!). The other thing that happens as objects come closer is that our visual accommodation changes.

Another cue to distance perception, especially for more complex scenes in which there are multiple objects, is binocular disparity. That means that each eye records a different angle of the visual field. Yet another cue to distance is motion parallax. As you move from one location to another objects at various distances will move in a direction dependent on where you are fixating. Finally, it turns out that color and brightness can also have an effect on how far away something appears.

Another factor affecting perceived size is size constancy. This phenomenon results in objects of known size tending to appear constant in size regardless of their actual distance. So, for example, if you are looking at your friend and that friend starts walking away from you, the friend does not, at the same time, start to appear smaller, even though the visual angle subtended by that friend is getting less and less. Well, size constancy also depends on the distance and if it is large enough, known objects will appear smaller. If you have ever looked at the ground from a very tall building, you will have noticed that people on the sidewalks and cars in the streets look very small. Perspective also plays a part in perception of size.

In conclusion, despite our ability to judge distance and size differences in many cases, our ability is distorted by a wide range of subjective factors. What is really interesting is that size illusions affect only the visual perception, and not the senses which control our organs of motion. Thus, scientists presume that there are two kinds of visual connections – one directly concerning visual perception and the other involving motory control.

In the following pages we will explore some of the things that affect our ability to estimate comparative lengths, sizes and shapes, and examine some geometrical properties that induce those deformations. But

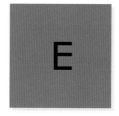 

Quick Color Eyesight Test
Close one eye and stare at the two colored squares each containing the letter E. If one of the Es seems darker you may need a pair of glasses! Do the test with the other eye too. This test is based on the chromatic aberration of the lens in our eye making red colors focus slightly behind the retina and green colors, slightly in front. In normal conditions chromatic aberration passes unnoticed, but a slight nearsightedness or farsightedness increases the irregularity, making a color go over the edges of a letter E.

He took my glasses off and he said, "Without your glasses, why, you're beautiful!" I said, "Without my glasses, you're not half bad either."
- Kit Hollerbach

what are the main errors in size perception? First, we tend to perceive any line or segment enclosed between two acute angles (less than 90 degrees) as shorter than it really is, and a segment enclosed between two obtuse angles (more than 90 degrees) as longer. The second most frequent error is that parallel lines seem closer to each other when they are oblique rather than displayed orthogonally. We will also take into consideration the so-called alignment illusions and perceptive distortions, whereby repeating regular background patterns can so strongly dominate other regular geometric shapes placed on to them, that they appear distorted.

Color perception

As the neurologist Sir John Eccles clarified once and for all: color doesn't exist at all in nature! Color only starts to exist when our perception systems produce the impression of 'color': light is perceived on the retina as a stimulus and is processed into a perception of color in our brain. In substance, colors are already illusions in themselves.

That's why color sensibility is individual and color taste differs from man to woman and even from country to country (different cultures have different terms for colors, and may also assign some color names to slightly different parts of the spectrum). Those variations in color sensibility between man and woman may have been especially important in very early times, when humans were hunter-gatherers. Enhanced color perception would have allowed women, who were traditionally gatherers, to better discriminate among colored fruits, insects and foliage.

Yes, we don't all have the same sensibility towards colors... Some people can't distinguish certain hues or colors at all. This is a problem of 'color deficiency' (commonly known as 'color blindness') and is most commonly due to an inherited condition. Color deficiency seems to occur in about 10 per cent of males of European origin and about one-half of 1 per cent of females. Red/green color deficiency is by far the most common form and causes problems in distinguishing reds and greens. Another color deficiency, blue/yellow, also exists but is rare, and there is no available test for it. Total color deficiency (seeing only in shades of gray) is extremely rare. There is no treatment for color deficiency, nor is it usually the cause of any significant disability. However, it can be very frustrating for individuals affected by it. General assessment of color vision can be made with the Ishihara card test.

Color serves a special function in the processes of vision. Our ability to analyze and process colors is a result of having three types of cone receptors in the retina, which have different light wavelength sensitivities: the short (blue), the mid (green) and the long-wavelength (red) cone receptors. But seeing a color involves making comparisons, because all that a single cone receptor can do is capture light and analyze its intensity... it tells nothing about color! Because of the overlap between the sensitivity ranges, it is not possible to stimulate ONLY the mid-wavelength (green) cone receptors: the other cones must be stimulated to some degree at the same time. To see any color, our brain must compare the input from the other cone receptors and then make many other comparisons.

So, on your PC screen, blue, green and red lights are sufficient to create the impression of color. But is it possible to create the illusion of color using only two different single-color lights? Edwin Herbert Land, the inventor of the 'Polaroid', demonstrated that we can perceive nearly the full range of colors by viewing superimposed two monochrome slides: one illuminated with red light and the other with white light. Land's experiment confirms that the color sensibility of a particular category of cone receptors is relative and depends on the other cone categories. Land also demonstrated in another experiment, using colored patches, the color constancy, i.e. our brain that condition our way to see the world around us.

Color adaptation or assimilation is the tendency of the eye to adapt in seconds to most prevailing light sources. Because of this effect, the eye can, in turn, accurately identify the colors of objects under changing lighting conditions. Adaptation will be seen by a person traveling in a vehicle with tinted windows; if, for instance, the tint is blue, the landscape will at first seem suffused with a blue cast but, as the eye quickly desensitizes itself to blue, the view will soon reassume its normal coloration.

Lightness constancy – Objects that are viewed under different lighting conditions usually 'look' the same to us. For example, a white T-shirt will look the same whether it is brightly lit on a sunny day or dimly lit on an overcast day. This is despite the fact that the wavelength of light that reaches the retinas in each case is different. This is explained

"I want you to realize that there exists no color in the natural world, and no sound, nothing of this kind; no textures, no patterns, no beauty, no scent..."
- Sir John Eccles

by the fact that the brightness of an object's surroundings usually changes in proportion to the change in brightness of the object itself.

After-image is a negative or complementary 'ghost' of a color seen after prolonged stimulation of the eye. An after-image occurs by staring first at a black spot on a white surface for around 20 seconds, then shifting one's gaze to a black surface; a floating

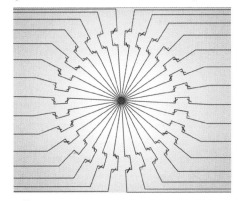

Follow My Eyes
Stare at the center of the geometric picture shown here. Keeping your gaze fixed on the central blue spot, move your head backwards and forwards several times. What happens? The blue concentric circles appear to rotate in opposite directions! Photocopy the picture and paste it on a rectangular piece of cardboard. Then, keeping the image 30cm away from your eyes, give a swinging movement. What do you see now? The concentric circles seem to expand or shrink, like the aperture of a camera, depending on the swinging direction you give to the image.

white spot will be seen briefly. The after-image of a red spot would be blue-green, that of a blue one would be yellow-orange, and that of a violet spot would be greenish yellow. After-image effects involve the optical nerves. An optical nerve is composed of millions of neuronal fibers which connect the retina to the brain by decoding the stimuli of the retina into three different signals: light difference (black/white) or luminance, red/green color difference, and blue/yellow color difference. When you stare at a red square for 20 seconds or more, the cells of the optical nerve which transmit the **presence of red AND the absence of green** will be under tension and will be saturated; consequently, when the stimulus suddenly disappears, the brain will interpret this stimulus cut effectively as the **absence of red AND the presence of green**. A green square will therefore appear in your visual field… It's like a short flip-flop effect. Interestingly, most standards for television transmission use a very similar decoding system, with one luminance and two chrominance channels.

A curious effect called retinal rivalry may be obtained by stimulating both retinas, each with a different color. For instance, when blue glass is placed before one eye and yellow or red before the other, the two independent monocular fields fight for supremacy; vision appears alternately in one color and then the other, and the brain has great trouble resolving the images.

Simultaneous color contrast is an effect in which the contrast between adjacent colors is enhanced by the eye. The effect is particularly strong with a pair of complementary colors, such as red and green or orange and blue. If these colors are put together in tight patterns, the resulting contrast is so strong that flicker will occur and the eye may experience considerable discomfort. Simultaneous lightness contrast is an effect in which a color of given brightness will look darker on a light background and brighter on a dark background. Simultaneous contrasts depend on lateral inhibition of our visual system.

Some photoreceptors of the retina are activated when they detect light, while others are activated in the absence of light. These two types usually encircle each other and are spread throughout the retina, creating receptive fields. Often, light can fall onto both light and dark photoreceptors, causing the two regions to compete with one another. One part of the receptive field wants to become active while the other part does not. This competitive interaction is called lateral inhibition. Because of this antagonistic nature of receptive fields, perceptual illusions, such as the Herman or Lingelbach grid illusion, can occur or when we look at certain patterns containing contrasting colors.

Since warm (reddish) colors tend to advance in our visual field and cold (bluish) colors tend to recede, objects painted in red and orange will seem to be slightly larger than those painted in cool blues and greens. Red cars or buses may seem larger than they actually are, but a room painted in red will seem more confined than a blue one. The reason for these effects is chromatic aberration, a problem associated with lenses (including the one used to focus light in the human eye), in which light is refracted by different amounts according to its wavelength. As a result, yellow is the only color perfectly focused by the normal eye, with red focused slightly behind the retina and blue slightly in front. The second reason may be that associative elements come into play. For example, blue may seem to recede because of the association it has in our memory with distance (the sky, sea, distant mountains…). The value (relative lightness or darkness) of a color also affects our perception of the weight of an object.

In the following pages you will experience some effects related to color including: color and lightness illusions, neon color spreading effect, scintillating grid effect, Kanisza illusion, Boynton filling-in phenomenon…

Anomalous motion illusions

How is it possible to create the illusion of motion with geometric and static images? There is a branch of modern art named Op'art (short for `Optic art') which is concerned with such effects. Op'art paintings often play with optic interference and moiré to create illusory colors and motion. The originator of

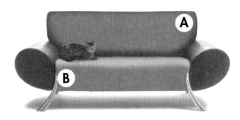

Grey Sofa
Is the gray zone in A darker than the gray zone in B? The gray zones in A and B have exactly the same hue. We tend to perceive the gray zone in A to be darker. This experiment shows that the perceived brightness doesn't rely only on the amount of light that reaches the eye from the observed object.

"What is mind but motion in the intellectual sphere?"
- Oscar Wilde

Op'art was Victor Vasarely, a Hungarian artist. But Bridget Riley is perhaps the best known of the op'artists. Taking Vasarely's lead, she painted a number of works consisting only of black and white lines. Riley's paintings depict an unreal geometric world which frequently give the impression of movement or color.

Anomalous or apparent motion illusions are based on alternating optical contrasts (clear/dark, vertical/horizontal, left/right) to create a perturbation, like a visual overload perturbing the retinal circuits, which can, among other things, make our eyesight flicker. There have been a number of analyses of the apparent motion illusion. The most obvious interpretation seems to be in terms of what computer vision scientists call `optic flow'. Until now, we can count roughly four different families of relative movement or kinetic effects:
- phantom movements, like moving flows, scintillating and popping-up patterns;
- floating images (such as Ouchi illusion);
- rotating shapes (B. Pinna and G. Brelstaff illusion);
- self-moving and spontaneous rotating shapes (peripheral drift illusion).
Let's go deeper into two of them…

Pinna rotating illusion

The Pinna-Brelstaff rotating illusion consists of two (or more) concentric rings of slanted lines or geometric shapes. When an observer moves towards it, the two rings of geometric patterns appear to counter-rotate. The illusion is optimal when there is a 66 degree orientation difference between elements composing the inner and outer rings. This illusion can be nulled by introducing a physical rotation opposite to the direction of the illusory motion. In other words, geometric patterns that are actually counter-rotating are perceived as stationary. Three factors may cause this illusion: the luminance profile, the angular direction of the shapes and the bad integration of motion signals in our brain.

The peripheral drift illusion

This illusion was first described by the scientists A. Fraser, K. Wilcox, and J. Faubert. The most famous peripheral drift illusion, designed by A. Kitaoka, is called Rotating Snakes. It consists of concentric repeating patterns of white, yellow, black and blue that evoke a striking illusion of motion. What makes this illusion so interesting is that you are experiencing movement in the periphery, although you realize that the moving objects are not moving at all! We've discovered that if we retouch Rotating Snakes using the 'threshold application' of Photoshop, it reveals the image's darkest point and the illustration then shows radial patterns of optic flows.

While peripheral vision demonstrates movement over the entire field of the display, focusing on one particular part of the illusion shows that it is stationary. There are no definite answers to explain this phenomenon but the main characteristics of the illusion are:

1. Illusory motion appears in the direction from a black region to the adjacent dark-gray region or in the direction from a white region to the adjacent light-gray region.

Colors indicating the directions of illusory motion: black to dark-gray or white to light-gray.

2. It occurs well in peripheral vision. The object we fixate appears to be stationary.

3. It occurs well with stimuli of edges. Stimuli of smooth luminance profiles give weak illusions.

4. It occurs well with fragmented or curved edges. Stimuli made up of long edges give weak illusions.

5. It may be generated by involuntary halting eye movements.

Some illusory moving patterns work better on a computer screen (because of the luminance), so you can try scanning them and watching them on your PC.

Ambiguous, bistable and completion figures

Does the mind represent the world accurately and unambiguously? Actually, ALL inputs to the brain are, to some degree, 'ambiguous', allowing multiple interpretations. That's the reason why we have poets, artists, singers… The capacity to perceive and give different meanings to our environment is part of our human condition.

What are *ambiguous figures*? Briefly, ambiguous figures are 'two pictures in one' – looked at one way, we see one thing (e.g. a vase), but looked at in another way, we may see something else (e.g. two faces in profile). They are somewhat similar to *bistable figures*, in that there are two ways to interpret each one, but bistable figures don't contain different subjects; they contain just one subject that flips perspective (e.g. Necker's cube).

One of the most antique ambiguous images, representing two confronted boars' heads that also form a facing panther head, was coined on early Lesbos money (Greece) about 2,500 years ago.

Ambiguous figures have long fascinated artists, children and others who enjoy surprises. The most famous example of ambiguity in painting is the *Mona Lisa*'s smile by Leonardo Da Vinci. In his book, *The Story of Art*, Ernest Gombrich reports: "Even in photographs of the painting we experience this strange effect, but in front of the original in the Paris Louvre it is almost uncanny. Sometimes she seems to mock at us, and then again we seem to catch something like sadness in her smile." Ambiguous figures, aka *equivocal images* or *metamorphic images*, are of special interest in the investigation of thinking. This is because they exemplify the fact that sometimes the same perceptual input can lead to very different representations, suggesting that the brain is actively involved in interpreting what we see rather than passively recording it. The curious aspect of ambiguous figures is that once you have perceived both figures, it is impossible to focus on only one without the other popping into your vision from time to time. Our brain, in fact, resolves visual ambiguity by means of oscillation.

Ambiguous figures include *figure-ground illusions*, ambigrams and what we will call completion figures. Figure-ground illusions are illusions that swap around the main figure and its background. Ambigrams are graphic words or sentences that can be read in more than one way. Completion figures are patterns which the mind rather unambiguously interprets in a particular way despite the fact that the input is incomplete in relation to what is typically 'perceived'.

A certain style of completion figures, called *droodles*, was used in the late 50s to entertain puzzle enthusiasts and magazine readers. These cartoons were rather abstract line drawings accompanied by an implicit question:"What is it?" A punchline (usually a funny description) finally made the cartoons obvious. Completion figures and droodles are based on the **pareidolia** (payr-eye-DOH-lee-uh), an innate human tendency to impose a pattern on random or ambiguous shapes. Astronomer Carl Sagan claimed that this tendency to see faces in tortillas, clouds, cinnamon buns and the like is an evolutionary trait. He writes: *"As soon as the infant can see, he recognizes faces, and we now know that this skill is hardwired in our brains. Those infants who a million years ago were unable to recognize a face, smiled back less, were less likely to win the hearts of their parents, and less likely to prosper. These days, nearly every infant is quick to identify a human face and to respond with a goony grin."* (Sagan, 1995.)

Giving meaning to abstract forms can also be a way to exercise our visual thinking skills. Even Da Vinci heartily recommended this method of invention as a practical technique for *"opening the mind and putting it upon the scent of new thoughts"*. He once wrote: *"If you look upon an old wall covered with dirt or the odd appearance of some streaked stones, you may discover several things like landscapes, battles, clouds, uncommon attitudes, humorous faces, draperies…"*.

Impossible figures

Impossible figures are a development of the `simpler' ambiguous figures. When we observe a two-dimensional picture on paper, we often interpret it as a

Temple of Colors
Examine the pale purple rectangles on the Greek temple. Are they of the same shade or do some rectangles appear darker than others? They are, in fact, all the same hue. Objects tend to be darker when placed on a clear luminous background and vice versa.

three-dimensional figure. This insistence to view objects as three-dimensional can lead to interesting perceptual problems.

An impossible object, also called an undecidable figure, is an object that cannot exist according to the known laws of physics but has a description or representation suggesting, at first sight, that it can be constructed. Generally, impossible objects depend on the ambiguous connectivity possible in line drawings. We like to call these improbable objects Frankenstein figures because they are made by matching together two or more different points of view of the same object, or by extending and blending together the perspective of one object with another one. Some impossible figures are not immediately obvious. You have to focus your attention on a particular zone of the representation of the object – the line of fusion of the contrasting perspectives – to understand that it cannot be realized. The paradox is that if you consider a sufficiently small zone of the drawing, the oddness disappears. That is to say, the 'impossibility' is not here, or there – it is something about the object as a whole. This paradox could perfectly illustrate the philosophical principle which says that "the whole is something completely different than the sum of its parts"...

The more normal the impossible object looks, the more fascinating it becomes! Impossible figures aren't created to baffle your eyes – their structure should appear coherent and logic – they are designed to confuse your mind. The 'undecidability' of these figures invariably rests on them being interpreted as two-dimensional projections of what would be an impossible higher-dimensional object. Artist Maurice Escher is notable for many drawings that feature undecidable figures, sometimes the entire drawing being an impossible figure. Oscar Reutersvärd, another important artist, has conducted a lifelong exploration into the world of impossible figures, producing a prodigious body of work during his long career. Notable modern undecidable figures include:

- Impossible cube;
- Penrose stairs;
- Penrose triangle;
- Blivet (or devil's pitchfork).

We should not forget to add Mickey Mouse ears to the list. Yes, his ears do not follow the basic rules of perspective. Children and adults alike are so accustomed to the current aspect of this cartoon character that they don't notice that his ears are actually impossible figures!

But impossible figures have a long

history... In 1025, an unknown European artist unintentionally drew the first example of impossible figure art (three impossible pillars), in an illustration known as 'Madonna and Child – Adoration of the Magi' from the prayer book of Henry II kept in Munich library. Another example of an impossible artistic object (a gallows!), was painted by Pieter Brueghel in *Magpie on the Gallows* (1568). However, the first artist who 'deliberately' misuses perspective to create an absurd and impossible landscape is the famous English artist William Hogarth (1697-1764), whose artwork Perspective absurdities formed the frontispiece to J. J. Kirby's book *Dr Brook Taylor's Method of Perspective Made Easy in Both Theory and Practice* (1754). This book was intended to teach people how to draw in perspective, so the caption asserted:"Whoever makes a design without the knowledge of perspective will be liable to such absurdities as are shown in this frontispiece".

Paradoxes: verbal illusions and vanish puzzles

Illusions and perceptive puzzles based on misconceptions and misperception can be useful to interest people in exploring and following logic and mathematical topics. On the following pages, you'll be able to experience the persuasive powers of the images and learn how a picture can sidetrack your senses of reasoning! We will also take the opportunity to deal with self-referential images and graphic words.

What exactly are *vanish puzzles*? Vanish puzzles (we've renamed them 'stereophanic puzzles') have existed for five centuries, but still continue to amaze everyone! They can be of two types: figurative and geometric. Figurative vanish puzzles involve the rearranging of parts of a puzzle representing a scene with a series of elements (persons, animals, etc), so that, once the rearrangement is completed, an element of the scene disappears (or re-appears). Geometric vanish puzzles involve either the apparent disappearance of a part of their surface or an apparent reducing of their area when the pieces of the puzzles are re-arranged. The first example of vanishing area puzzles was discovered in the book *Libro d'Architettura Primo* by Sebastiano Serlio, an Italian architect

"What if everything is an illusion and nothing exists? In that case, I definitely overpaid for my carpet."
- Woody Allen

of the Renaissance, even though Serlio didn't notice that any area had actually vanished. The first description and explanation of this paradox was found in a math puzzle book with a very long title: *Rational Recreations in which the Principles of Numbers and Natural Philosophy are Clearly & Copiously Elucidated, by a Series of Easy, Entertaining, Interesting Experiments among which are all those Commonly Performed with the Cards* (1774) by William Hooper.

Because of their visual impact vanish puzzles are really striking, but their mechanism is quite simple: the part (figure, surface) which disappears is simply redistributed differently on the remaining parts of the puzzle; confirming Lavoisier's law which says "In nature, nothing is created, nothing is lost, all is transformed". Then, the magic is only based on the **visual persuasion** that the puzzle is really different after manipulation. Vanish puzzles are just one aspect of perception puzzles... In this book, you will find new games and magic tricks directly involving visual perception or visual memory.

A *self-reference* occurs when an object refers to itself. Reference is possible when there are two logical levels of interpretation which can sometimes interfere with each other (contradiction).

The philosopher Heraclitus of Ephesus is recognized as one of the earliest philosophers who used self-reference in his dialectic, as in his statements:

– Nothing endures but change.
– Expect the unexpected.

The elliptical logic of his aphorisms earned Heraclitus the epithet 'Obscure'. Many self-referential paradoxes are hidden in our everyday language ("there's something I want to tell you BEFORE I start talking..."). They are like optical illusions – they seem normal but when you examine them closely, the incongruity becomes obvious! Some self-referential statements can lead to paradoxes. The most famous self-referential paradox, called 'the Liar Paradox', is an argument that arrives at a contradiction by reasoning about a Liar Sentence. The classical Liar Sentence is the following:

– This sentence is false.

Actually, 'this sentence' is neither true or false. Experts in the field of philosophical logic have never agreed on the way out of the problem despite 2,300 years of attention...

GALLERY I

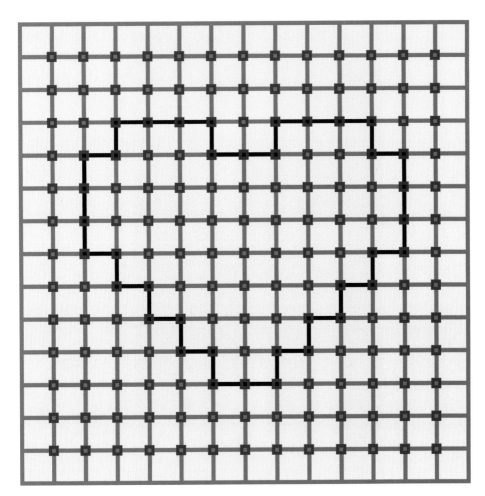

Neon Heart

Can you see an orange heart with a bright border? View the picture from a good distance. The color in the background is perfectly uniform, the apparent orange color is created by the interaction of the black lines with the yellow background, and the white halo by the interaction of the blue lines with the small dark squares.

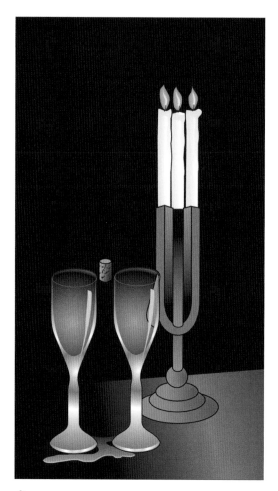

Just Two Anomalies
There was a party, but where is the bottle? Do you see another oddity?

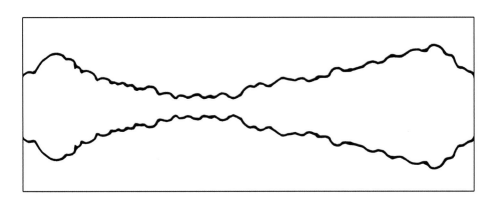

Cloud Test

With just one stroke transform these clouds into a forest.

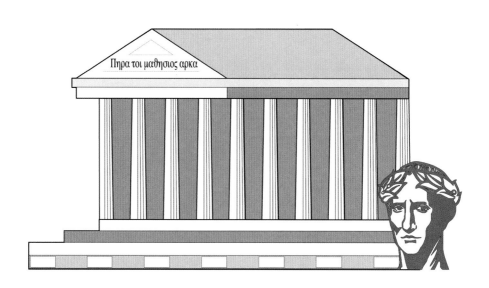

Greek Temple

Cut the puzzle (copy it first!) into two pieces in order to make a column of the temple vanish when the pieces are perfectly rearranged. Impossible?

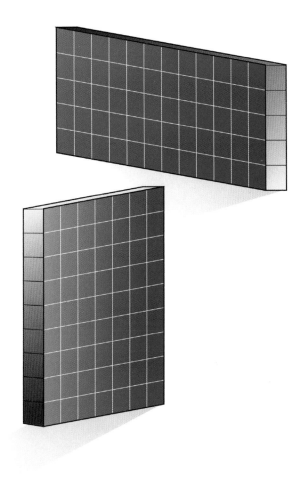

Low Walls

Are the blue surfaces of the two walls different? Can you calculate their area?

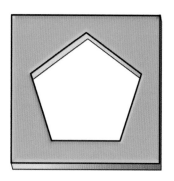

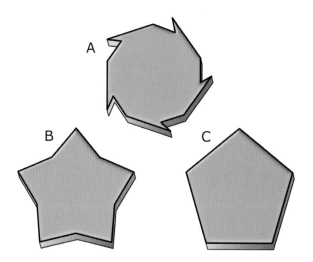

Visual Fitting Test
Which shape (A, B or C) fits exactly into the pentagonal hole?

Impossible Tearings

Take a strip of paper and make two incisions in it as shown in the picture. Hold the strip by its ends and pull in order to break the strip. What is the probability that the central piece marked with an X falls out: 1/3, 2/3 or 3/3?

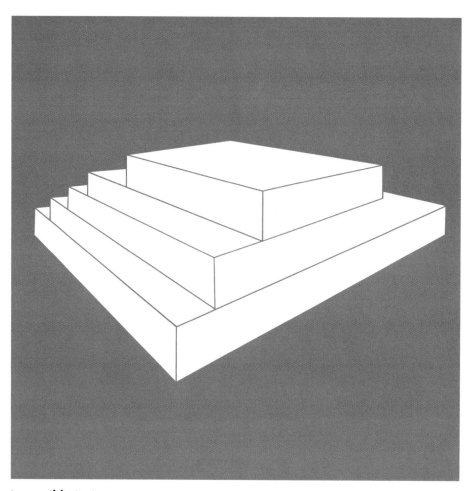

Impossible Stairs

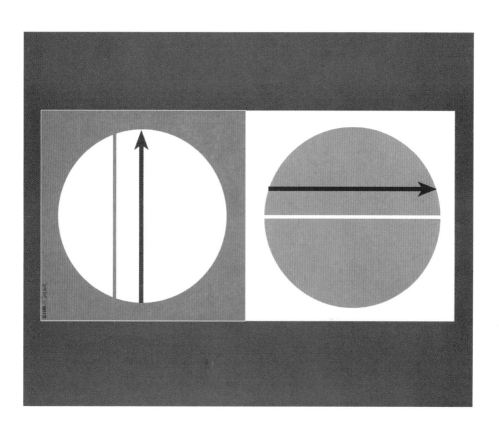

Arrows

Is the red arrow longer or shorter than the blue one?

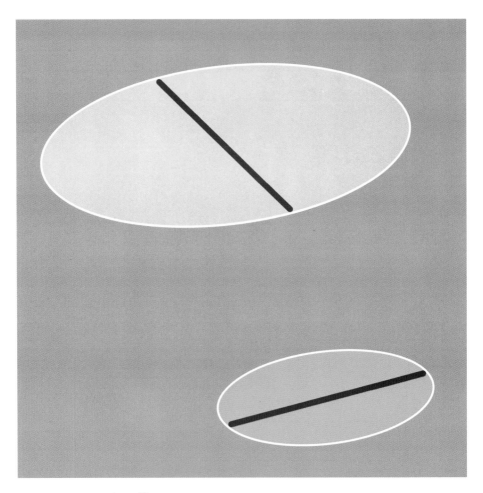

Sarcone's Deceptive Ellipses

Which line seems longer, the red one or the blue one?

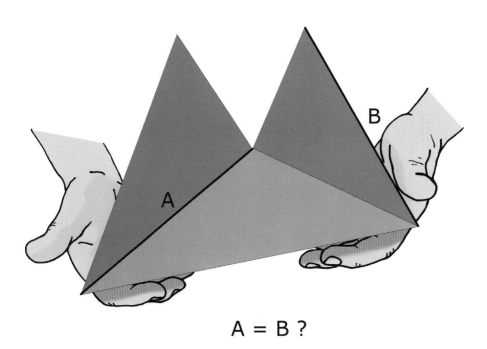

A = B ?

Line A = Line B?
Are lines A and B really the same length?

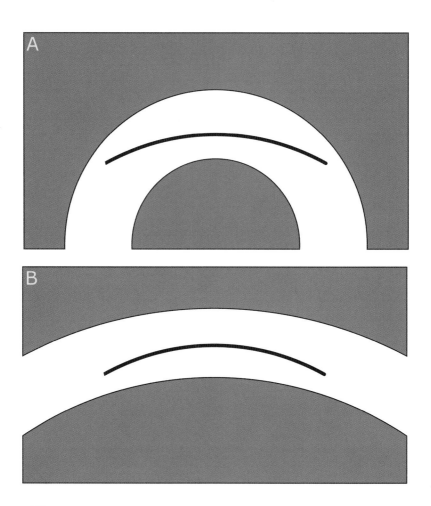

Curved Lines

Which arc segment has the greatest radius of curvature, A or B?

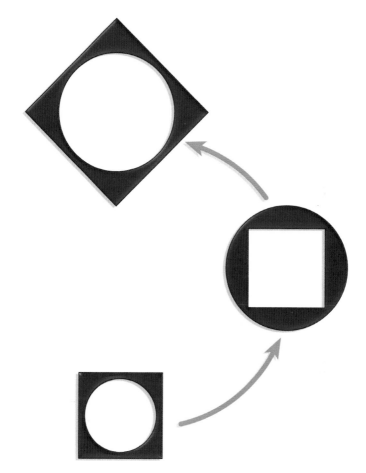

Fit It In!
Do the shapes fit inside each other like Russian Matrioshka nesting dolls?

Geometrical Visual Effects

Interesting geometrical effects with concentric squares.

A = B ?

Line A = Line B?
Are lines A and B the same length?

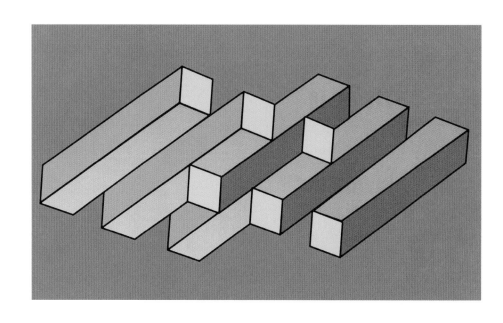

Impossible Rods

Which group of rods is on top in the picture and which one is underneath?

humans are likened to prisoners chained in a cave, unable to turn their heads and thus to see any real objects. All they can see are shadows of objects projected by a light source on the wall of the cave. What the prisoners perceive, therefore, are just shadows and echoes cast by objects that they do not see at all. Such prisoners would mistake app ... (shadows) for reality.

But wh... is vision? What is the v... ion is the most creativ... a human being is capable of. See... icting the world on the living ca... our mind. As we depict well only w... ve really know, our mind is both the canvas and the artist. In this creative process, the eyes represent nothing ot... an a medium with which our min... ets and 'reconstructs' the reality ... s. The poet Novalis said: "the ey... perficial organ". In fact, we wil... he real world because ... pendent of our body and o... es, vision isn't quite the 100 per cent natural process that folk may think... It relies for a large part on *learned skills* that are helpful in interpreting our near environment, but can sometimes deceive. That's why the study of visual illusions and mental fallacies is important: they reveal the magic and the limits of our perception (or

imagination do we need to understand how we truly perceive ourselves and how others perceive us? Try this experiment: scan a photo of yourself and, with the help of a photo retouching software, flip it horizontally to create a mirror image and print it. Now compare this image with the original photo. Which of the two faces do you prefer? Show ... s to a friend, and ask which ... e prefers. You will prob... r image and your frie... n. It's a question of habit – we ... t which we are used to... Two ... the same person! But the illus... also of the mind; especially when we believe we can control our thoughts. Try NOT thinking of a polar bear. Did you m... it, or did the polar bear lumber slow... ur mind? Now try to think of a ... en man and think qui... m 1 to 5... Then a nu... We bet you thought of ... example is when imaginatio... collide' – it is always imagination which leads the way. It is easy to walk across a board laid flat on the ground but, with all the will in the world, quite impossible to walk the same plank suspended between two buildings ten floors up. The consciousness is one of the greatest mysteries of the brain. Many actions – walking, catching the bus,

Illusory Magnification

The pac-man-like shapes create a rectangle which has an illusory magnifying glass effect, in fact the text within it seems much easier to read.

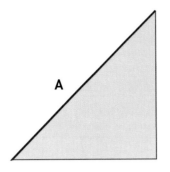

A = B ?

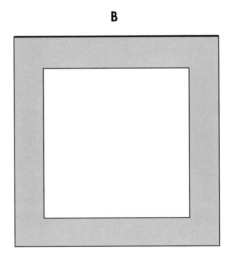

Side A = Side B?
Which side seems shorter, side A or side B?

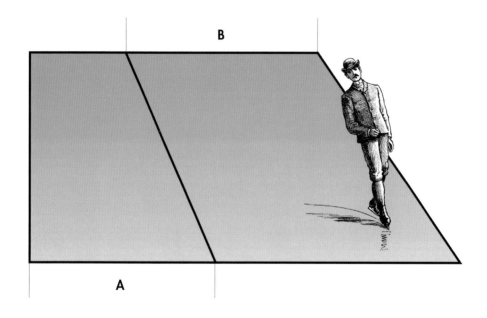

B

A

A = B ?

Line A = Line B?
Line B seems longer… but are you sure?

The upside-down
sentence is *TRUE*

Visual Logic Paradox
This is either an ambigram (turn the page upside-down) or a self-referential
paradox. Now ponder whether the sentence is true or false.

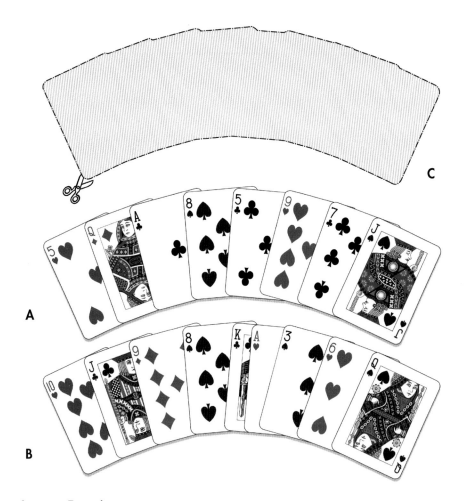

Jastrow Experiment

Ask your friends which of the fanned-out sets of cards is the widest: A or B? The fact is both sets are the same size and width. To prove it, reproduce the fig. C and cut out the dotted shape, which coincides perfectly, when superposed, with the outline of both sets of cards.

GALLERY I NOTES

Page 24
The bottle is concealed between the two glasses. The other oddity is that it is impossible to say if the candelabra has two or three sticks.

Page 25
Here is a forest reflected in a mountain lake.

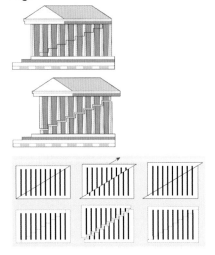

Page 26

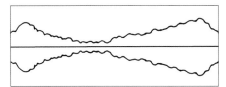

Page 27
Visually, the first wall seems to have an area of (12 x 5 =) 60 square units; and the second one, an area of (7 x 9 =) 63 square units. But actually, the blue surfaces are identical in shape and size, even though they look different! This illusion is related to the "crossing parallelogram" illusion. To find the real area of the blue surfaces, called parallelograms, you have to multiply their **base** by their **height**.

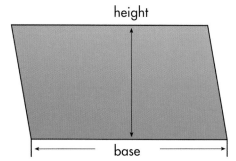

Page 28
Shape A!

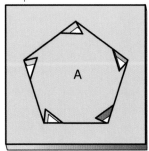

Page 29

The probability that the central piece marked with an X falls out is 0/3! This is the illustration of an improper use of probabilities for a physical event. We are simply deceived by our common sense.

Page 31

Red arrow = blue arrow!

Page 32

The blue line is longer than the red one. Measure them!

Page 33

Yes, they are.

Page 34

In fact, the arc segments are identical. The context in which the arc is placed determines its appearance.

Page 35

No. None can be fitted into another!

Page 37

Yes, they are the same length, despite the fact they look different. This is a variant of the Ponzo illusion.

Page 38

It is impossible to determine which group of rods is on top. These are just impossible figures.

Page 40

The hypotenuse, A, of the triangle seems shorter than side B of the square. However, they are the same length.

Page 41

In fact, line A = line B.

Page 42

This contradictory sentence is not resolvable in conventional logic systems.

THE UPSIDE-DOWN SENTENCE IS TRUE
But if the upside-down sentence is true, this sentence is false (contradiction); Etc...

Etc...
this sentence is true (contradiction);
But if the upside-down sentence is false,
THE UPSIDE-DOWN SENTENCE IS FALSE

But not all self-referential sentences are paradoxical: consider 'this sentence is true'.

GALLERY II

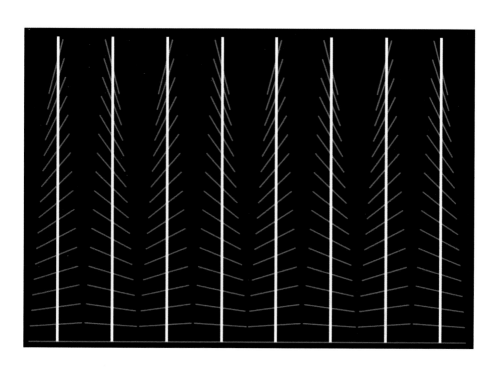

Distorted Lines
Do the lines tend to bend in at the top? No; it's just an illusion!

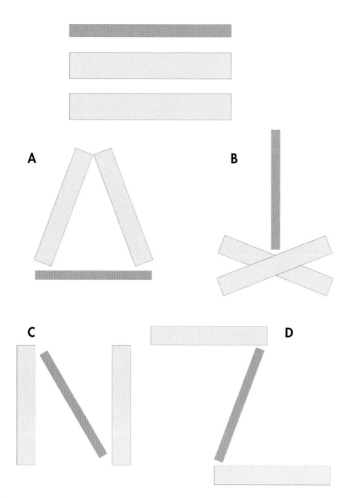

Paper Strips

Make two sets of three paper strips as shown in the picture and form, in turn, figures A and B. Strangely, in configuration A the thinner paper strip looks smaller than the thicker paper strips; in B the effect is reversed! Finally, make figures C and D; curiously, the paper strip in the middle looks longer in configuration D.

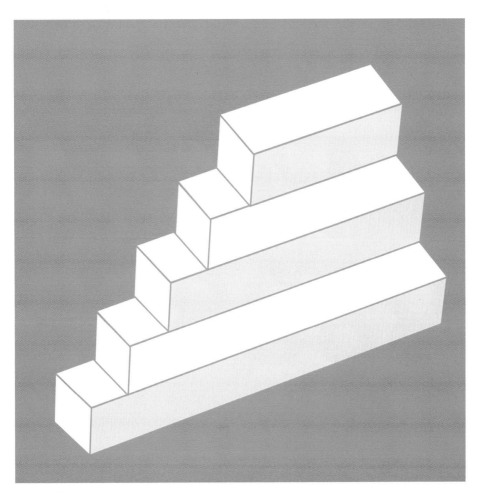

Impossible Stairs 2

444444

888888

Fours and Eights

Consider the two rows of numbers. Are all the fours the same thickness? What about the eights?

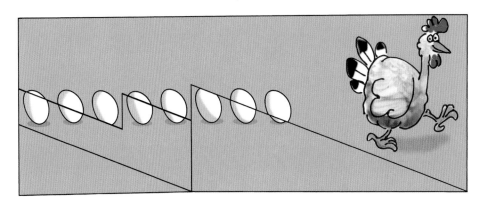

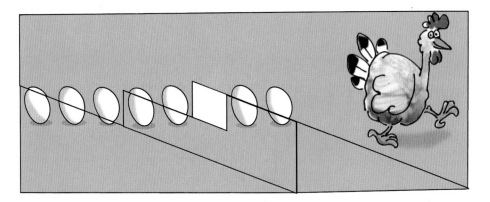

Befuddling Chicken and Eggs Puzzle

Who 'stole' the egg from Chiquita, our favorite chicken? As you can see in the four-piece puzzle at the top, there are eight eggs... But, if we move some of the puzzle pieces around, an egg disappears along with a portion of the puzzle. But the missing portion doesn't have an egg on it! How does this work?

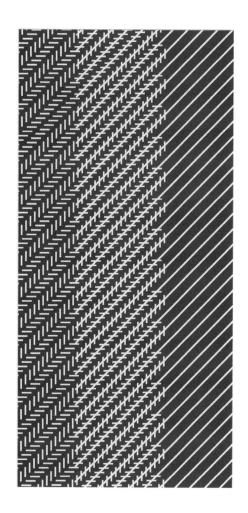

Zöllner Revisited
The conjunction of parallel lines and sets of oblique strokes creates an interesting distortion illusion.

Tracing Star

First, photocopy the star. Then, take a pencil and trace a line within its borders while you are looking in the mirror at your drawing. You can hide the drawing with a book as shown in the picture. Find it easy?

Seal or...?
Can you see how to transform a marine mammal into a flying animal?

Solitude

Is the old lady really alone? How many people are with her?

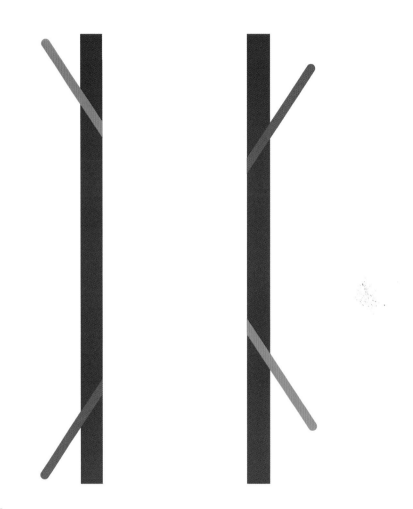

Aligned?

Which line segments aren't aligned correctly to form a straight line, the magenta or the green ones?

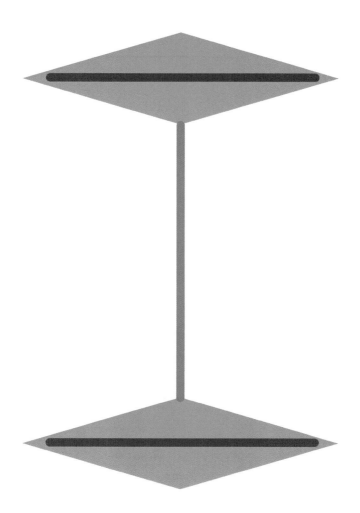

Lines

Is the blue line longer than any of the red lines?

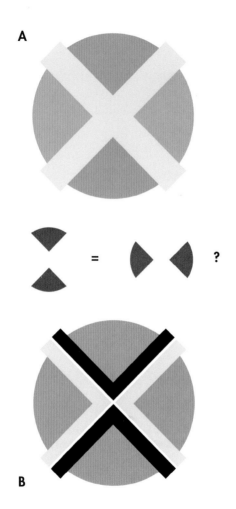

Sliced Colors

Consider both colored figures in A and B. In which case (A or B) are the vertical green slices the same shade as the horizontal slices?

Visual Memory Test

Concentrate on both red and green symbols for ten seconds. Relax… Now select one of the playing cards – any of them – and firmly concentrate on it. Memorize your card, then turn the page over!

Magic Cards

Believe it or not, the card you selected has been removed from the assortment and turned over. Right?

A

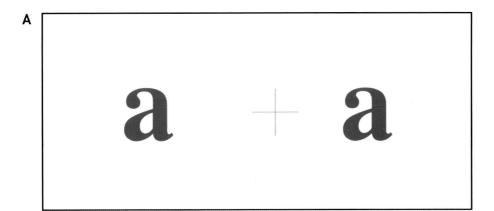

B

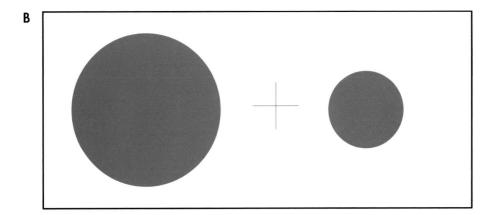

Bold the A

To enlarge one of the 'a' letters shown in diagram A, stare at the dots in diagram B for about 20-30 seconds, then look at the letters 'a'. You should see a letter becoming larger and bolder! (The experiment works better under bright light).

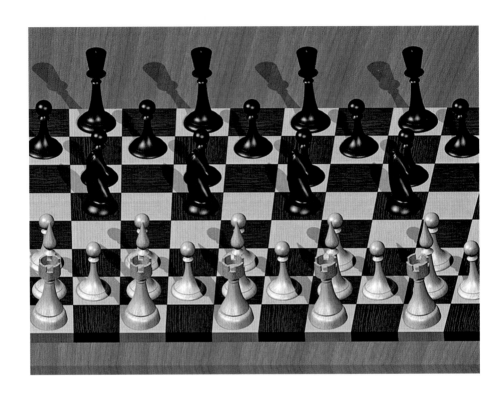

Autostereogram: 3D Chess

In order to see the image in 3D, bring the picture close to your eyes, so it touches your nose. At this distance, your eyes cannot focus on the image and they focus somewhere BEHIND the image. Now, slowly move the image away from you, while trying to keep your eyes out-of focus until you see the 3D effect. This illusion involves *binocular parallax*: depth perception arising from the different perspective each eye perceives of a three-dimensional scene. Image courtesy of 3Dimka.

Parallel or Not?
Are the yellow lines bulging outwards?

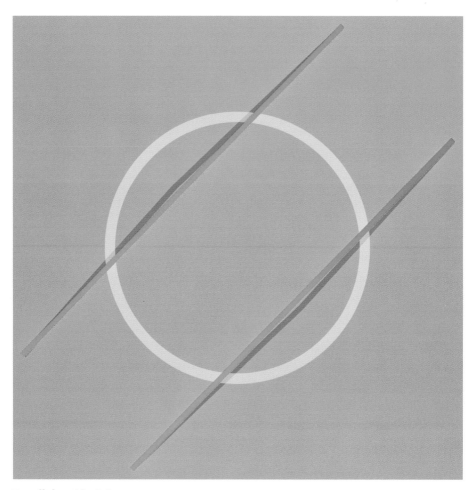

Parallel or Not? 2
Are the green lines straight and parallel to each other?

Floating Thoughts

Do you see the shapes of floating thinking men and women? It's just your imagination…

Master of Numbers

Look at this mosaic made with a random arrangement of numbers from a distance. What do you see?

Impossible figure?
What's wrong with this 3D structure?

GALLERY II NOTES

Page 50
The three 4s on the right are slightly larger, while the 8s are all the same thickness. The second set of 8s on the right was just turned upside-down.

Page 51
Reassembling puzzles which include triangular pieces may lead to paradoxical conclusions! In this particular case, we have two paradoxes in one when both triangular pieces of the puzzle are inverted:
1. a substantial portion of the puzzle seems to be missing;
2. an egg has vanished.
Of course, apparent gain or loss of area is offset by a complementary loss or gain elsewhere in the puzzle. The loss of the small surface is due to the fact that the bases of the triangles aren't perfectly aligned to form a continuous straight line at the bottom of the puzzle. In figure A, the point where the triangles meet is slightly retracted, whereas in B it is protruding. The area of the 'missing' surface in B is simply redistributed within this prominent line. And what about the missing egg? This is a Columbus egg. By switching the triangular pieces of the puzzle, the egg

doesn't disappear at all – a fraction of the image is redistributed among the seven eggs that remain. Can you see that the seven remaining eggs in B are slightly longer than the eight eggs shown in A?
This puzzle, involving the vanishing of a surface as well as the vanishing of a graphic element, is an original novelty invented by mathemagician Gianni A. Sarcone. You may have heard of him somewhere!

Page 53
Tracing a drawing with the help of a mirror can be very confusing for our procedural memory. The procedural memory is our motion memory. When performing something with procedural memory, one is not consciously aware of exactly how one is performing each individual movement or how to combine the movements. Becoming aware of these things can disrupt a well-learned skill. Now, when you try to draw something by looking in a mirror, you have to inhibit and reverse all that is associated with vision and motion control (and as you have experienced yourself, the first time it is very, very difficult!).

Page 54
Just turn the image upside-down and you will discover a toucan.

Page 55
You can see the presence of five faces in the tails of the cats.

Page 56
The green segments aren't properly aligned to form a straight continuous line.

Page 57
The lines are all the same length. This is a Müller-Lyer illusion variant.

Page 58
In A the vertical slices are different from the horizontal slices.

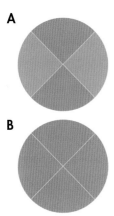

Pages 59–60
This trick is simply based on visual memory. Hint: people concentrate on the selected card but not on the surrounding playing cards.

Page 61
This is an original after-effect experiment.

Page 63
No; they are perfectly straight and parallel to each other. This distortion illusion is induced by the cross in the background.

Page 64
Even though they seem to bulge inwards, they are perfectly straight and parallel to each other. This distortion illusion is induced by the circle in the background.

Page 65
There are no really determined shapes in the drawing; just lines and illusory figures!

Page 66
The face of the famous physicist Albert Einstein will appear.

Page 67
See picture below

incorrect

correct

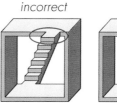
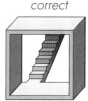

GALLERY III

Good Vibrations

Do you see some converging vibrating flows? No, you aren't seeing things; it's just a natural lateral inhibition effect.

The Lonely Dancers

Are they really lonely?

Impossible Eight-Point Star?

Cut slits in two single square paper sheets so that, when the sheets are interlaced, they form this eight-pointed star figure.

Magic letters

Read the word on this picture. Then, try to read it from a distance (2-3 meters away). What does it spell?

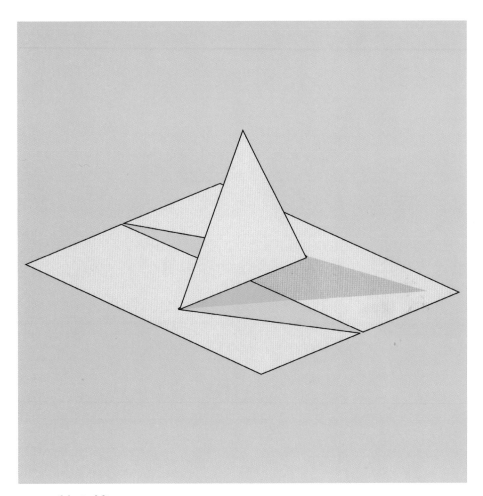

Impossible Foldings

Can you reproduce this pyramid-like figure just by cutting and folding a single piece of strong paper? (You cannot cut the paper into two or more different pieces.)

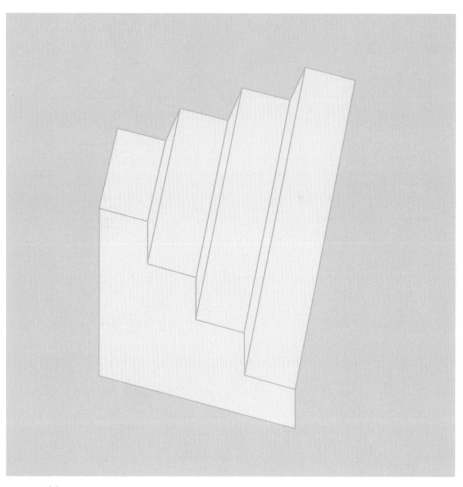

Impossible Stairs 3

Living Eyes
Wherever you are, this face seems to follow you with its eyes.

Gray Gradations

Color gradations can affect the alignment of regular objects. In the picture, the squares are perfectly aligned and parallel!

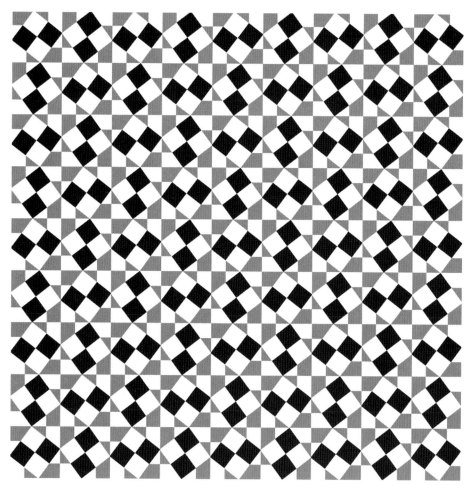

Round Corners?

The checkered small squares seem to have wobbly, round corners. Squares tend to lose their evenness when assembled in regular sets.

Boing Visual Patterns

An interesting visual effect of coaxial circles and ellipses is created by placing a negative arrangement of concentric black and white circles with an 'invert blending mode' on an alignment of black and white stripes. Changing the thickness of the stripes alters the image dramatically, as illustrated above.

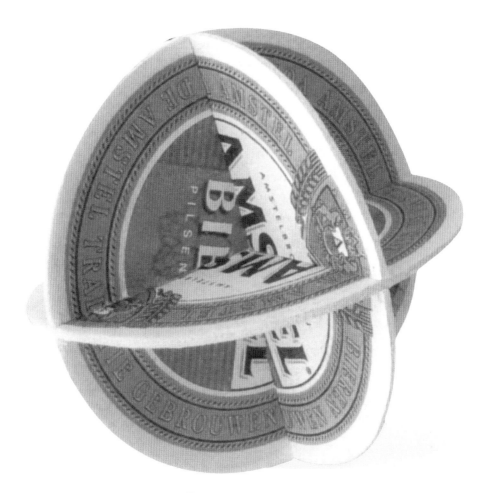

Make a Magic Cardboard Ball

Take three circular mats or pieces of stiff card and try to assemble them as shown in the picture. The figure is made by cutting and interlocking three single pieces together without glue or adhesive of any kind. Is this figure possible?

Moving Concentric Circles

Concentric regular arrangements cause visual perturbations. The circles appear
to vibrate and turn. To increase the rotational effect, move the page gently in a
circular fashion. This kind of illusion is one of the oldest apparent motion illusions.

Moving Radial Pattern

Radial patterns can induce visual perturbations. The image seems to shimmer when the page is moved slightly. If you move your eyes around the spokes you may even see color appear.

Magic Top
Move the picture from side to side to make the top spin.

Moving Square

The inset square seems to move independently of the background and the surrounding pattern. You can enhance the effect by shaking the picture slightly.

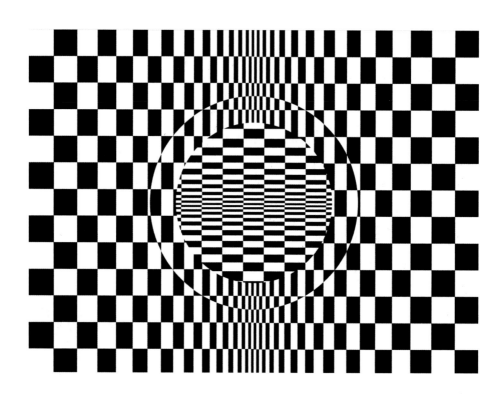

Floating Disc

Observe the image and concentrate on the central disc, while shaking the image slightly. The circular shape appears to separate from the rest of the picture and levitate above the checkered background.

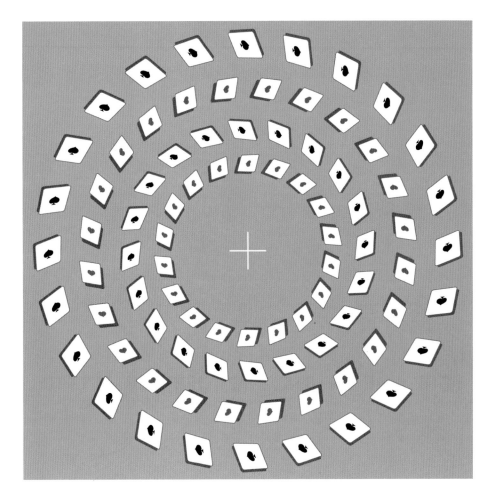

Rotating Circles

The circular sets of playing cards seem to counter-rotate when you move your head backwards and forwards, keeping your focus on the cross in the center of the image. Do you notice something odd?

Horizontal Fluids
The wavy colored 'neons' seem to wink and flicker just like real Christmas light-chasers! How is that possible?

Fill the Van

Is it possible to fit all these boxes into the van? If not, which pieces cannot be included?

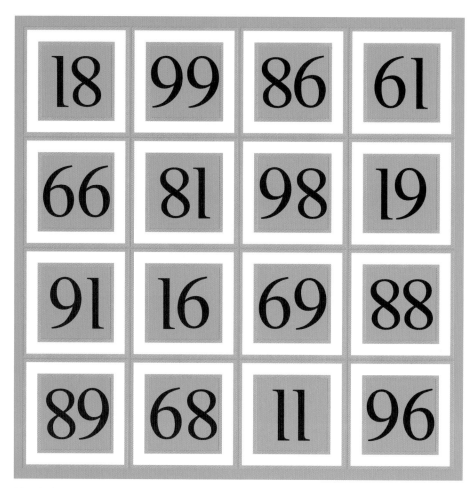

Magic Magic Square

Magic squares are squares filled in by aligned numbers with the characteristic that the sum of the numbers of each row, column, and diagonal is the same. The square featured on this page is a magic magic square. Why?

Euler Color Patchwork
Look at the picture from a certain distance and check which colors are in the patchwork.

GALLERY III NOTES

Page 72
A woman's face can be perceived at the center of the illustration. This is an ambiguous figure-ground illusion.

Page 73
Here you can see the cuts in the paper sheets which allow you to form an eight-pointed star.

Page 74
When the picture is seen close-up, the fine details dominate and you can read the word "learn", but when you observe it from a distance, the more blurred tones become more coherent and the word "teach" appears.

Page 75

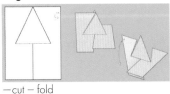

—cut — fold

Page 77

A

B

The effect is due to the ambiguity of the face. In fact, we have modified a real unidirectional face (A) by inverting symmetrically the top of the face around a vertical axis. The result (B) is a bidirectional ambiguous face. Our judgment of where a person is fixing his gaze is influenced by set. In this particular case there are two possible sets; in just one image.

Page 81
Here is the secret: cut as shown in the example before you interlock them.

Page 84
Illusory motion is induced by the visual contrasts of the top and its background.

Page 85
We tend to perceive the inset square and the surrounding pattern as two independent fields even though they are on the same plane. The surrounding pattern is interpreted as a 'frame of reference' and usually tends to be

stationary. The visual contrasts of the inset square and the surroundings in the picture seem to confuse the motion detector of our visual system.

Page 86

This is a variant of the Ouchi illusion. When you make eye movements while following the picture, the visual contrast of the foreground and background patterns may induce illusory motion at the edges of the central disc. This kind of illusion is thought to arise from retinal motion signals (the motion detector of our visual system). Another interesting observation: the boundaries of the ring which include the Ouchi disc appear to shine slightly, like a neon.

Page 87

The circular set of playing cards with the ace of hearts rotates faster than the circular set with the ace of clubs.

Page 88

This illusion is induced by the alternating small dark strokes with the white background. The rapid movement of the eyes called "saccades" causes small shifts in the geometric position of the peripheral areas of the color neons producing repeated contrast reversals (afterimages) that could create the illusive visual flickering.

Page 89

Yes, the van can contain all the boxes.

Page 90

It is reversible. It remains a magic square even if you turn it upside-down! If you look at it from a certain distance, the corners of the small orange squares (containing the numbers) lose their regularity and seem to sharpen.

Page 91

The only colors featured in the patchwork are: cyan, yellow and magenta. The patchwork's background is made with sets of 4 squares colored in just 3 shades, onto which are accurately superposed concentric circles with the same colors. Many people see extra colors like green, orange, red, violet or blue… The phenomenon that is responsible for the apparition of the extra colors is known as "assimilation of color" (also known as the *Von Bezold spreading effect* or *Bezold-Brücke effect*) – when the areas of colors are very small, they take on the hue of the surrounding color.

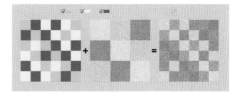

GALLERY IV

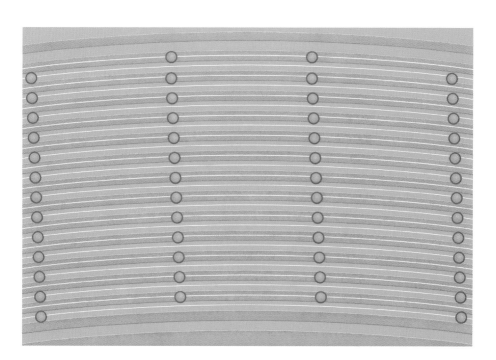

Aligned Dots?

It seems incredible, but all the dots are the same shade of pink and the dots that appear clearer are perfectly aligned with those which appear darker. Take a ruler and verify the situation for yourself! These illusions are induced by two factors: contrast of colors and the bended colored lines.

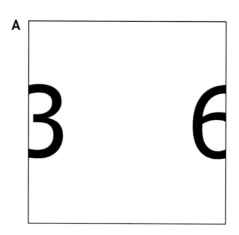

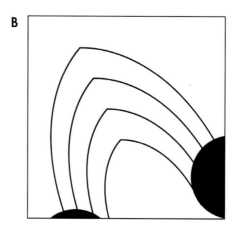

Droodles

What do images A and B represent?

3D Sundial
This picture of a sundial seems confused and flat. Close one eye and look along the direction indicated by the blue triangle at the bottom of the illustration, leaning the book back as you look. What happens?

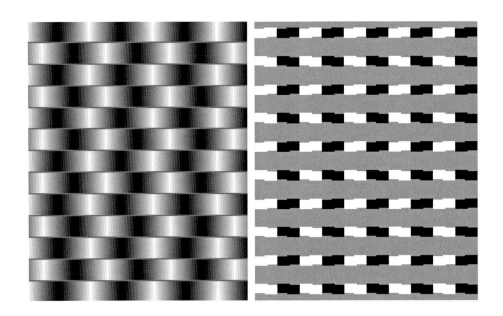

Distortion Effects
In the two pictures above, shades and square saw-tooth outlines induce parallel slats to appear divergent or convergent.

Self-Referring Word

This image represents a self-referential word (the word 'clock' with a clock inside). A self-referential graphic word is a word that encapsulates the thing it represents within itself, like: ei8ht, dOt, lllree, f1rst, para//e/... Can you determine why semordnilap is a self-referential word?

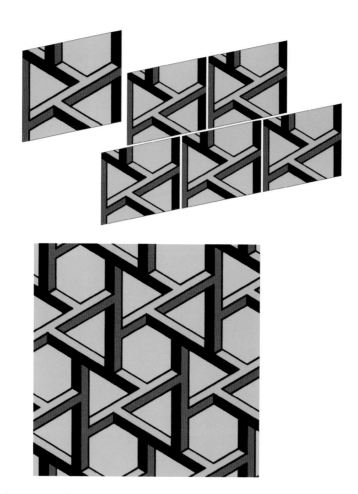

Impossible Figure Tiles

With the parallelogram tile, it is possible to assemble an impossible structure.

Triangularize It
Using these three 'blocks', form the representation of a pyramid.

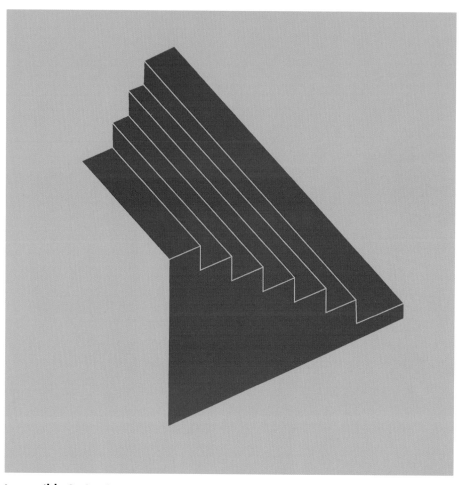

Impossible Stairs 4

Flashing Star
This is a peculiar Op Art (Autokinetic Optical Illusion) with a vibrating effect and a recursive *Droste effect* ("mise en abîme").

Bidimensional Temple

Observe the scene: there are several architectural absurdities!

Another hidden number?
Spot the 8 in the middle of this 8 of diamonds card.

Size distortion
Which pen is longer: the one on the left or the one on the right?

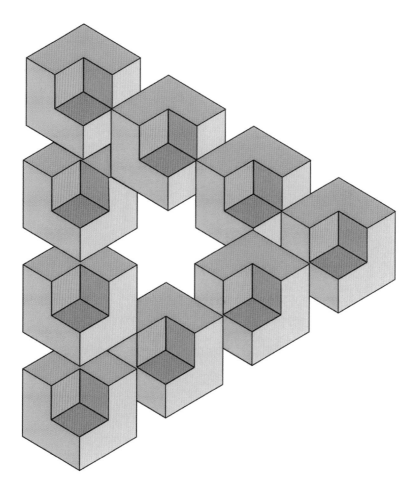

Cubic Tribar
In this impossible figure, called a tribar, do you see two sets of cubes or just one set of cubes with a small cube cut out?

Blues

The blue spots set on the darker background appear lighter than the blue spots on the clearer background. But all the blue spots have identical hues! This compelling visual phenomenon is described as simultaneous lightness contrast.

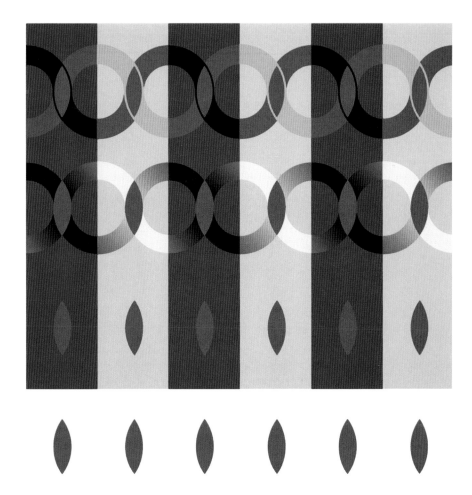

Braids of Shade

Three intriguing variants of simultaneous lightness contrast involving lenticular colored shapes (you can see at the bottom of the illustration how the lenticular colored shapes really appear). The two upper examples combine multiple color boundaries and lead to a strong illusion.

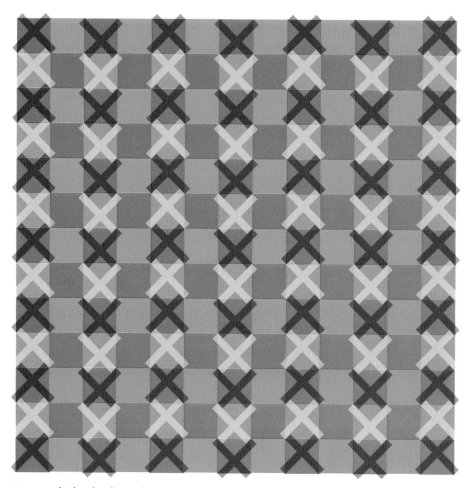

Distorted Checkerboard
Alternating cross patterns make the columns of the checkerboard diverge.

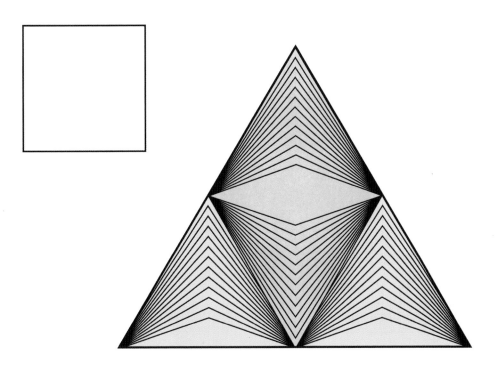

Find the Hidden Shape

Can you find the square in the triangle with your naked eye?

Deadly dazzles

What a dazzling pattern! The repetitive arrangement of contrasting lines and the eye saccades are responsible of the uncomfortable visual oscillations you may experience when watching this picture. In addition, an image is encrypted in the geometric pattern, can you spot it?

Old Trans-Siberian

Reproduce the card depicting an old Trans-Siberian train and cut it into three pieces. Then rearrange the rectangular card again in order to transform this seven-carriage train into a six-carriage one.

A

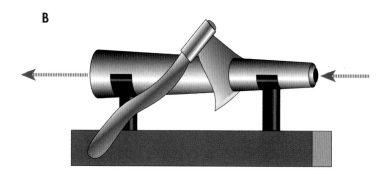

B

Slashed Telescope

The telescope shown in figure A is split by an axe into two pieces (figure B). Explain why it still works and why it is possible to see through the axe.(Hint: the axe is not transparent! It is just a question of reflections.)

A Midsummer Day's Dream
Just enjoy this picture which contains this absurdity.

GALLERY IV NOTES

Page 96
Droodle A is a trombone player doing some stretching exercises before a performance. Droodle B is part of a spider's legs while it stands on a mirror.

Page 97
You will soon notice that the upright stick in the center of the sundial (the pointer) rises (and shrinks in height) all by itself.

Page 99
As semordnilap is `palindromes' written backwards, it's a self-referential word!

Page 101

Page 103
An image exhibiting the Droste effect depicts a smaller version of the image within itself in a seamless recursive manner. In theory, the main subject continues deeper into the picture ad infinitum, the recursion is however limited by the fixed resolution of the picture but can repeat as an infinite loop in animations. The pulsating effect of the picture is due to the repetitive design that alternates optical contrasts and to the involuntary eye movements called "eye saccades".

Page 105
The contours of the diamonds create an imaginary 8, as depicted in the picture below. Once you see it, you will never unsee it!

Page 106
Our intuition about perspective strongly influences what we see. When we see two objects with the same "apparent" size, the one that appears to be farther away is thought to be larger. Though the pen on your right side appears larger, both pens are actually the same height. This is a variation of Ponzo illusion.

Page 107

The image combines two illusions in one: an impossible figure together with an ambiguous figure.

Page 108

The observation that a color looks darker when set against white than when set against black has puzzled scientists and philosophers for two millennia, yet there is still no consensus as to exactly why it happens. Interesting observations and comments on this subject are provided by scientists Edward Adelson (lightness induction) and Alexander Logvinenko (lightness-shadow invariance).

Page 109

All the lenticular colored shapes are of the same shade, but we see lighter and darker lenticular shapes. We encounter a similar effect in everyday life: the screen of the television and of the PC aren't black at all, nor can black be created by the electron beams. But when you switch on your television you can see all the colors, black included!

Page 110

All the columns are perfectly parallel and aligned. This illusion is related to the Zöllner illusion.

Page 111

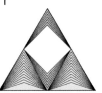

Page 112

A grinning skull is encrypted in the center of the geometric pattern.

Page 113

The steam train will lose a wagon depending on the way pieces A and B of the puzzle are reassembled.

Page 114

The trick lies in the four mirrors concealed in the telescope's prop.

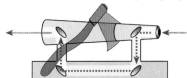

GALLERY V

Good Vibrations
Pulsating concentric diamonds? No, perfect concentric squares. This illusion is related to the Fraser illusion also known as "twisted cord illusion".

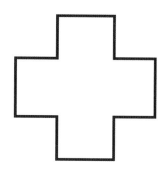

Find the Hidden Shape 2

Find the cross in the square!

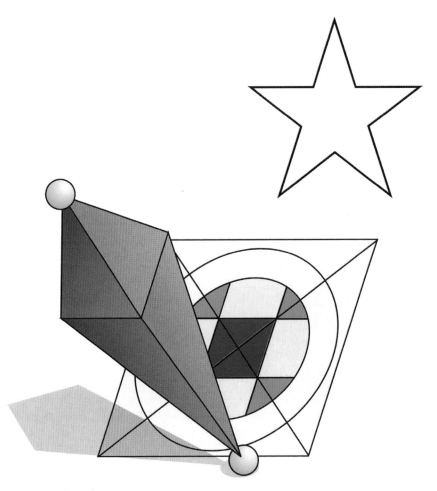

Find the Hidden Shape 3

Follow your star... Find it in the pattern.

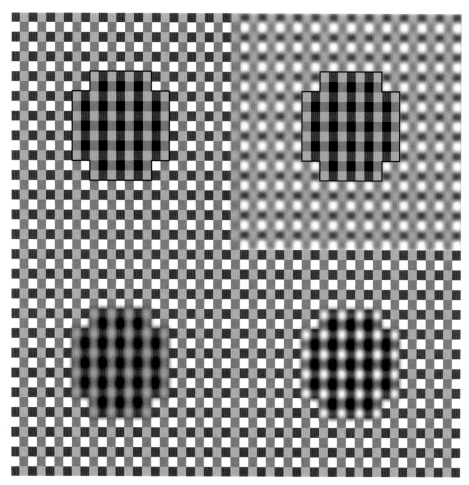

It floats!

Using only squares, it is possible to create patterns that evoke an apparent swinging sensation. Move the page slightly to and fro and the inset cross-like patterns will appear to move and 'float' relative to the checkered background. Some patterns will even move and hover more than others.

Divergent Crosses
Each pair of columns, made up of black and red crosses, seem to diverge.

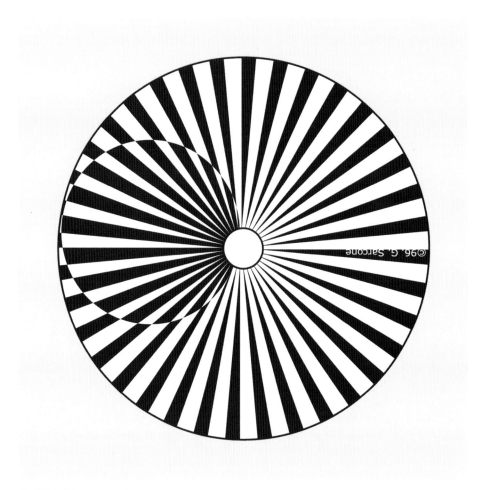

©96, G. Sarcone

Artificial Spectrum Top

Reproduce this circular pattern and paste it on to a piece of cardboard, then cut out the disc. Push a short, pointed pencil through its center. You now have a top with magic properties. Spin the top and you'll see subjective colors while it rotates.

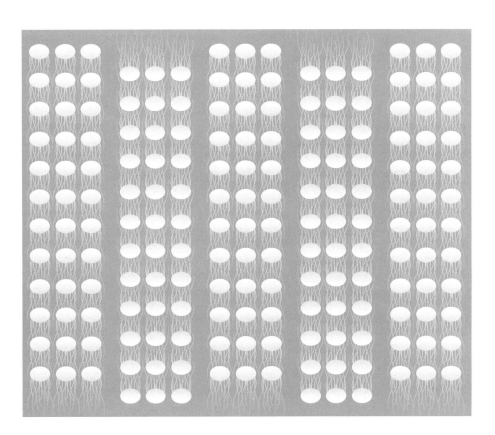

Moving Jellyfish

Stare at the image and imagine that the blue is the sea. Concentrate and cast your eyes around the groups of jellyfish and they will start to move in opposite directions.

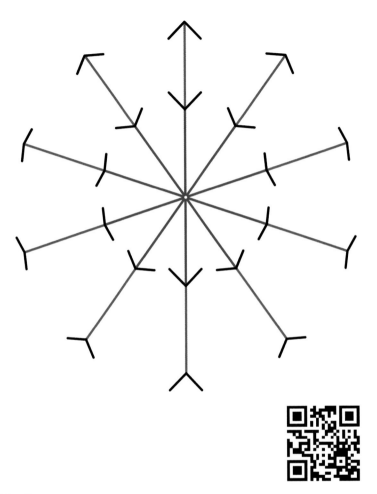

Size Distortion
Are the red segments and the blue ones the same length? Point your smartphone on the QR code and scan it to see online an animated version of the illusion.

Hypnotic Vibes

This is an Op Art with kinetic effects: Do you perceive the reddish portion of this design to be pulsating? Curiously enough, some people can even synchronize the virtual pulsations of the picture with the beat of their own heart. This Sarcone's Op Art is presented in many "Museums of Illusions" around the world.

Does it fit?
Is it possible to join the pieces together?

Magic Pile

Which coin, balanced on its edge, exactly matches the height of the stack of one-cent pieces?

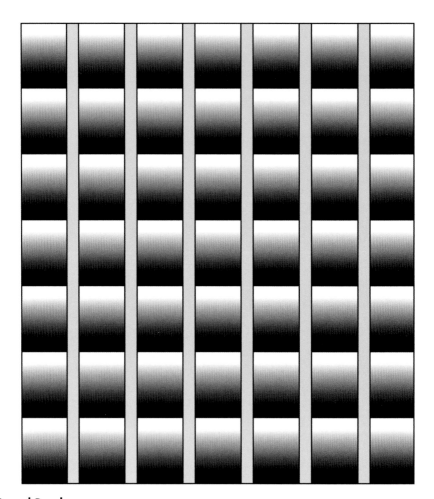

Unreal Bamboos

The dark gray boundaries which segment the 'bamboos' don't actually exist. The 'bamboos' are perfectly straight and parallel.

Yellow Lines

Are the yellow lines perfectly straight?

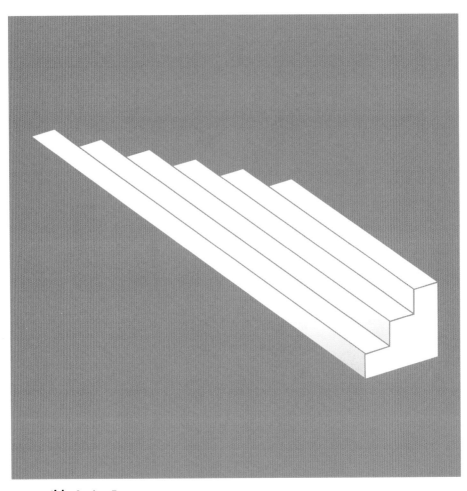

Impossible Stairs 5

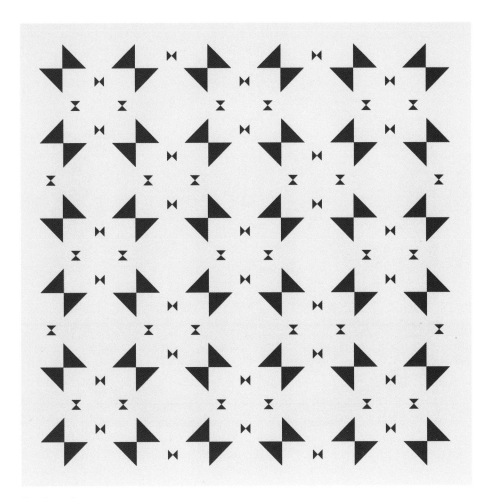

Kanisza Squares

How many perfect squares do you perceive?

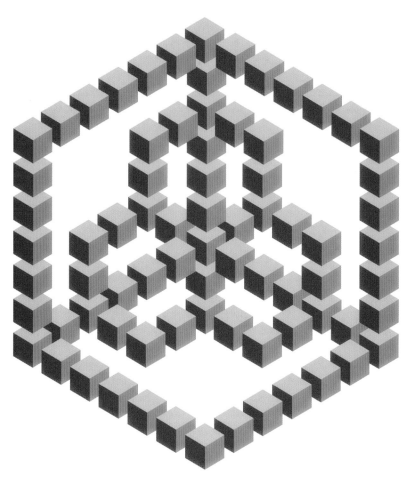

Impossible Cubic Structure

Just a neat cubic 3D structure…

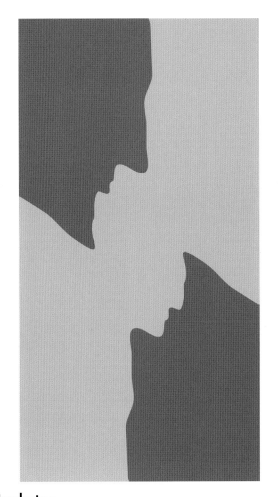

Listeners and Conductors
This is a figure-ground illusion. How many people do you perceive on this page?

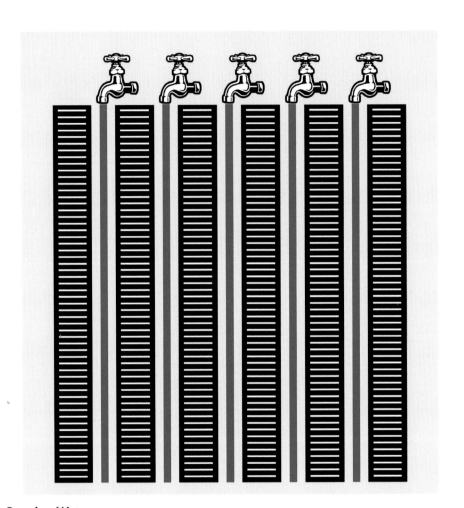

Running Water

Do the blue lines twist up and down like a water flow? Please turn off the faucets once you've experienced the illusion!

Moving Brands

If you concentrate on the circular colored bands, you may see a vibrating fluid moving around and, without thinking about it, you will soon enter a deep, peaceful, hypnotic trance, without any effort… This illusion is ideal for hypnotizers!

GALLERY V NOTES

Page 120

Page 121

Page 122

Just by replacing the white squares of the background pattern within the cross with black squares is sufficient to induce a sensation of apparent movement. This happens mainly because our brain interprets the cross-like patterns as being different and thus dissociated from the background. These illusory motion effects are related to the Ouchi illusion.

Page 123

This illusion is related to the Zöllner illusion.

Page 124

The 'color' observed with such rotating discs does not exist. If the disc is rotated in one direction 'colors' of red to blue may appear. If the disc is rotated in the other direction, the colors appear in the reverse order. Colors obtained with this top are subjective colors or – using a scientific term – pattern-induced flicker colors. The effect observed depends on the intensity of the light source, the speed of rotation and the design and distribution of the black lines. Observation in bright sunshine gives very satisfactory results. There isn't a complete and certain explanation concerning the observance of subjective colors.. Lateral inhibition and the different rates of stimulation for the color receptors in the eye are clearly involved.

Page 125

This illusory motion is related to the central drift illusion. The factor that induces this illusion may be the difference in contrast between the inner and outer areas of the 'moving' objects (jellyfish).

Page 126

Red and blue segments are all the same length. Visually speaking, the red segments seem to stretch towards the lower part of the star-like pattern, while the blue segments seem to stretch towards the upper part of the same. This is due to the different aperture angles of the black arrowheads. This is a variant of the Müller-Lyer illusion with which the author won the "Best Illusion of the Year 2017", you can see an animated version of this illusion on youtube: https://youtu.be/_ChpQfcRDLQ

Page 127
The pulsating effect is due to the repetitive design that alternates optical contrasts and to the eye saccades.

Page 128
Yes, it is possible. It is just the instruction drawing that is wrong. Here, the correct picture is shown.

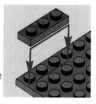

Page 129
One cent! This experiment demonstrates the difficulty of judging the real size of circular objects. Using real coins, you can demonstrate this trick to your friends.

Page 130
The illusion of dark gray spots is

induced by the sinusoidal gratings on the background. This is a classical case of lateral inhibition.

Page 131
The yellow lines are perfectly straight and parallel. Some visual illusions, like this one, occur in interrupted modular patterns.

Page 133
In the picture there are 13 small squares A, 13 squares B, 12 squares C and 12 squares D. In total, there are 50 squares.

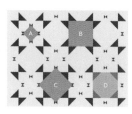

Page 134
This impossible structure, called multi-link cubes, was created by Vicente Meavilla Seguí.

Page 135
There are two enigmatic opera listeners (green) and two conductors (yellow).

Page 136
The illusion is due to lateral inhibition.

Page 137
Another lateral inhibition effect.

GALLERY VI

Unbuildable?

Take a piece of paper, cut it out and fold it to try to build the same structure shown in the photograph.

Rubber Ducks

Let's try an experiment with a color filling-in effect. Have a look at these cute rubber ducks from a distance of two meters (six feet). Most people only see yellow inside the outline of the ducks...

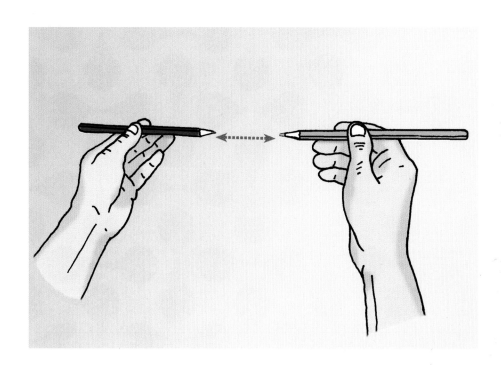

Elusive Pencils

Hold two pencils – a blue one and a red one – level in front of you. Focus on them. Slowly bring the tips of the two pencils together. No problems? Try the same thing with just one eye open. Easy? Not the same, is it?

Hypnotic Neon Lights

Do you see a pattern of large and small squares? The seemingly neon squares seem to pulse slightly when you concentrate on the image.

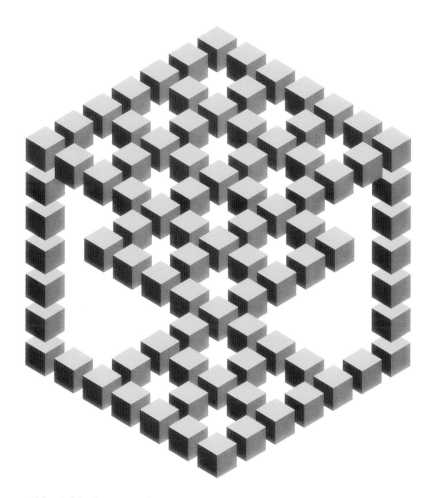

Impossible Cubic Structure 2
This is another curious cubic 3D structure.

The Ruler Attention Test

Something went wrong with this ruler... Can you guess what?

Fleeing Destiny
Does the golden fish move?

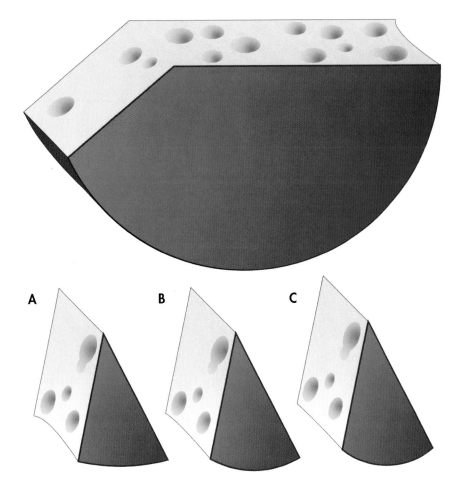

Who Cut the Cheese!
Which piece of cheese is cut from the semicircular Emmenthal cheese?

Mystery House

Find three weird perspective errors in the picture above.

GALLERY VI NOTES

Page 141

You will never be able to build the structure, as it is an "impossible figure". Impossible figures are two-dimensional figures (photos, drawings, etc.), which are instantly and subconsciously interpreted by the visual system as representing a projection of a real three-dimensional object. Notable modern impossible figures include:

- The Thiéry figure,
- The Necker cube,
- The Penrose stairs,
- The Penrose triangle,
- The Blivet (or devil's pitchfork).

Page 142

If you closely examine a rubber duck (without squeezing it) you'll notice that it is printed on a yellow rectangle (and the color obviously doesn't fill the exact inner surface of the duck!) Some colors, like yellow, have a low spatial resolution. That means it is difficult to perceive and define a determined yellow shape on a clear background. So, our visual system tends to constrain yellow colors in outlines.

Page 143

Each eye sees from a slightly different angle (binocular disparity). Both eyes work together to give us depth perception. You need depth perception for your brain to be able to judge distance. When you only use one eye, you lose depth perception. Depth perception is also dependent on colors; objects with warm colors tend to be seen as nearer than objects with cold colors.

Page 144

This optical illusion combines 'neon color spreading' with 'illusory contour' effect: not only do you perceive squares where NONE exist, but the squares also have phantom colors! Neon color spreading contains illusory contours, brightness induction, color assimilation, and perceptual transparency, all of which gives depth perception. Neon color spreading can also be observed in the Kanizsa triangle (page 156). Italian researcher Dario Varin first observed this phenomenon in 1971, but the name 'neon color spreading' was coined by H. F. Van Tuijl. The human ability to perceive a neon effect may be a remnant of the development of our power of sight under water at extreme depths, where light is very poor or absent.

Page 145

This impossible structure, called multi-link cubes, was created by Vicente Meavilla Seguí.

Page 146

There is an extra millimeter between 7.5 and 8, and one millimeter is missing between 9 and 9.5 (see the picture)

Page 147

Repetitive patterns with sawtooth shadings that imitate a 'motion blur' may appear to move in our peripheral vision which is highly sensitive to motion. Some researchers think that these kinds of illusory movements are due to the delays in luminance processing that produce a signal that tricks the motion system and induce "kinetopsia" (motion perception). That reminds me of the following anecdote:

Two Zen monks were arguing about a flag being blown by the wind.
One said: 'The flag is moving...'
The other answered: 'The wind is moving!'
The prior of the monastery happened to be passing by. He told them: 'Not the wind, not the flag; the mind is moving...'

This short anecdote serves to explain that the concept and perception of motion is sometimes ambiguous.

Page 148

We are sure you have answered `piece of cheese b', but you'd be wrong! The correct answer is `piece of cheese a'.

Page 149

The door is open simultaneously out and in (and that's not the only mystery here). The roof ends in another direction in relation to the house; and the leaves near the entry steps are ambiguous – we cannot see whether they lie on the ground or on the branches of the trees.

CLASSIC OPTICAL ILLUSIONS

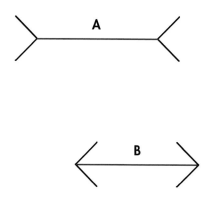

Müller-Lyer Illusion
line a = line b

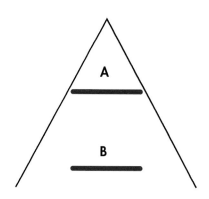

Ponzo Illusion
line a = line b

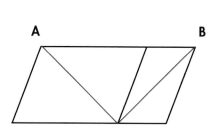

Sander Parallelogram
line a = line b

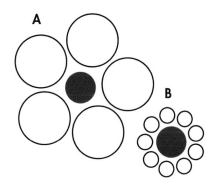

Ebbinghaus Illusion
equal red circles

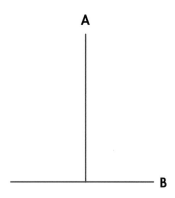

Fick Illusion
line a = line b

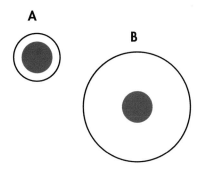

Delboeuf Illusion
equal red circles

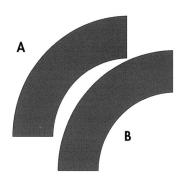

Jastrow Illusion
shape a = shape b

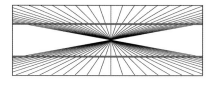

Hering Illusion
red lines are parallel

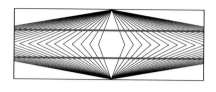

Wundt Illusion
red lines are parallel

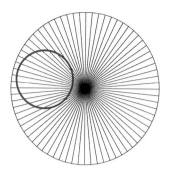

Orbison Illusion
perfect circle

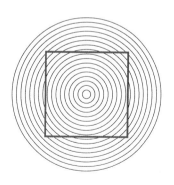

Ehrenstein Illusion
perfect square

Zöllner Illusion
parallel diagonals

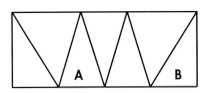

Fee Illusion
line a = line b

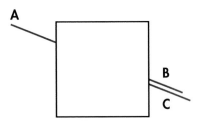

Poggendorff Illusion
segments a and b are aligned

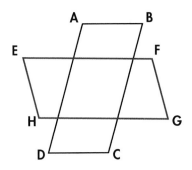

Crossed-parallelogram Illusion
parallelogram ABCD = parallelogram EFGH

Kanisza Illusion
phenomenal subjective white triangle

Fraser Illusion
lines are parallel

Café Wall Illusion
red lines are straight and parallel

GLOSSARY

Ambigram

A graphic word or sentence that can be read in more than one way. This can be achieved in several ways: by writing the word so that it can be interpreted in more than one way, or by making it meaningful when turned upside-down.

Ambiguous figures

Open to more than one interpretation. It means that an image as a whole can display different scenes, depending on the interpretation of the viewer.

Blind spot

We cannot see where the optical nerve enters our eye. We don't ever notice it because our eyes constantly make small movements and, above all, our mind just fills in the gap. It just guesses what should be there. The blind spot is actually quite big.

Color contrast and color assimilation

Color contrast refers to the change of hue when colors are perceived in the context of other colors. For instance, colors may look lighter or darker with respect to the background color, or even shift their hues into the direction of the complementary background color. When the areas of color in a pattern are very small, an effect opposite to simultaneous color contrast occurs: colors appear to become more like their neighbor instead of less like them.

Entasis

The slight convex curve used on Greek columns. This curve compensates for the optical illusion that a straight column seems concave.

Hidden images and Camouflage

Camouflage has been used for disguise in the natural world ever since predators developed eyes to track prey. In optical illusions, it is the art of hiding something elegantly in an image. Most often these are landscapes or natural scenes where extra animals or objects are hidden.

Impossible images

Impossible figures can be drawn on paper, but can't exist in real life.

Lateral inhibition

Some photoreceptors of the retina are activated when they detect light, while others are activated in the absence of light. These two types usually encircle each other and are spread throughout the retina, creating receptive fields. Often, light can fall onto both light and dark photoreceptors causing the two regions to compete with one another.

One part of the receptive field wants to become active while the other part does not. This competitive interaction is called lateral inhibition. Because of this antagonistic nature of receptive fields, perceptual illusions, such as the Herman grid illusion, can occur when we look at certain patterns.

Pareidolia
A kind of illusion or misperception where something meaningless is considered meaningful. For example, seeing a giraffe in a cloud.

Procrypsis
The ability to blend into the background. This environmental camouflage is most often seen with insects and many animals. Just think of walking sticks and those weird bugs that look like leaves.

Upside-down images
An upside-down or topsy turvy image is an image showing something meaningful when turned around. That can be one thing, or something completely different.

Recent works by the same authors
"illusion d'Optique" is the most jaw-dropping collection of optical illusion playing cards ever assembled. Housed in a wild, rainbow-sheen holographic case, you may feel like you are hallucinating before you even open the box.

Inside, you will find 54 eye-popping original designs created by a master of visual perception, Gianni A. Sarcone. Watch closely as colors change, shapes transform and static, printed ink seems to come alive. Sarcone has included updated versions of classic illusions, plus innovative new concepts he developed after years of study.

The playing card deck is available from Art of Play: https://www.artofplay.com/products/illusion-playing-cards

Sarcone's official optical illusion stores and art tutorials and collections
https://gianni-sarcone.pixels.com/
https://www.redbubble.com/people/giannisarcone/
https://www.behance.net/giannisarcone

ABOUT THE AUTHORS

"A world without problems is an illusion, so is a world without solutions." – G. Sarcone

Gianni A. Sarcone is a visual artist and author from Italy with over 30 years' experience in the fields of visual creativity, recreational mathematics and educational games. Much of his art blurs the line between cognitive science and communication. As Gianni puts it, his work is intended to "encourage people to look beyond what seems obvious and to open their mind to new emotions and dimensions."

A new kind of impossible tribar

His optical art is shown in many galleries and recently in the 'museums of illusions' all over the world.

He founded with Marie-Jo Waeber "Archimedes Lab", a free, independent and collaborative educational project whose main goal is to show mathematics in a different light and to make it accessible and enjoyable to everyone through original visual puzzles and games.

ⓦ giannisarcone.com ⓨ gsarcone ⓕ gianni.sarcone ⓘ g.sarcone

Archimedes Lab's website: https://www.archimedes-lab.org
Museums of Illusions' website: https://www.museumofillusions.com/